Hello!

I was a Stander and experienced how God restored my marriage.

My husband left the family, and I trusted God in restoring my marriage and family and after 16 months, my husband came back restored in faith. He actually said no one told him to come back home, but he believed the Lord changed his heart and sent him back home. I know the pain that is involved when a family is separated and the woman is left to pick up the pieces and raise the children alone.

This workbook is designed to empower Standers in understanding purpose and destiny through the challenges they encounter in their marriages and to build them to spiritually pursue all that God has for them while they wait in the promise of restoration.

During my Stand, God took me through a process of how to Stand righteously and that is why I've written this workbook to teach, mentor and coach you to understand Kingdom principles, your salvation to work and yield to Gods strategy for BREAKTHROUGH!

1 Samuel 30:8

Jacqueline Ani

Jacqueline Ani International
www.jacquelineaniinternational.org

The Standers Discipleship & Mentorship Programme

The Standers Discipleship, Mentoring & Coaching Workbook is a Kingdom Programme focused on empowering the Stander to Stand righteously for the restoration of a Covenant Marriage and to discover their purpose in Christ whilst Standing.

The Family Mountain has always been under attack because the adversary seeks to divide and conquer and he does this by removing the head in the home, sometimes it would be the woman in the home too. This programme is to empower, encourage and deliver those standing for marriage restoration and to take back the Family Mountain for God.

Kingdom people who have been attacked in their marriages must Stand for the deliverance of their spouse and children who have been deceived to abandon what God started.

God created woman to compliment and help man build. God created man to cultivate woman to help him to build the family. When the link is broken it affects the flow and purpose of that marriage.
The spouse standing must heal, align and work with God to restore their family.

The spouse who works with God for restoration is referred to as a Stander. The Stander has the assignment to Stand for the deliverance of their spouse and the restoration of the marriage and family as God Wills.

The Standers Discipleship, Mentoring & Coaching Workbook will prepare Standers to understand with clarity why the marriage has broken; heal in the process of Standing, learning how to Stand righteously and birthing purpose through the Stand preparing for restitution, restoration and reconciliation.

Website: www.jacquelineaniinternational.org
Email: info@jacquelineaniinternational.org
Founder/CEO – Jacqueline Ani
Jacqueline Ani International

Isaiah 58:12

Published by JA Publishing

46 Lullingstone Crescent

Telephone +44 7544255987

info@jacquelineaniinternational.org

www.jacquelineaniinternational.org

© Jacqueline Ani 2024

Jacqueline Ani asserts the moral right to be

identified as the author of this work.

Printed by Advanced Document Solutions, Uxbridge

ISBN 978-0-9548340-3-6

ALL RIGHTS RESERVED. No part of this book may be reproduced or transmitted in any form whatsoever, electronic or manual including photocopying, recording or by any informational storage or retrieval system without express written, dated and signed permission from the author.

Table Of Contents

MODULE 1

INTRODUCTION

An Introduction to the course
How to use the workbook
Journaling/Reflection

MODULE 2

IDENTITY IN CHRIST

Rediscovering Your Identity
Kingdom Citizenship
How to Stand with God
Purpose in the Stand

RESOURCES FOR MODULE 2

Mind Mapping
Problem Solving

MODULE 3

SPIRITUAL LOCATION

Understanding Seasons of Change
Understanding where you are in your Stand and how to navigate
Further healing in the soul
God's Expectation of You

RESOURCES FOR MODULE 3

Spiritual Gifts Workshop

MODULE 4

POSSESS YOUR POSSESSIONS?

The Three Categories of Gifts
Manifestation, Ministry & Motivational Gifts
How Your Gifts Supports the Body of Christ

Table Of Contents

RESOURCES FOR MODULE 4

Discovering the 3 Categories of Your Spiritual Gifts and applying them

MODULE 5

STIRRING UP YOUR GIFTS FOR PURPOSE

What Is In Your Hand?
Start from where you are with what you have.
Understanding Stewardship Launch what you have for the Kingdom.
Developing Leadership Skills

RESOURCES FOR MODULE 5

Launching Your Gifts Into Purpose (Practical Application) Researching who needs what you have

MODULE 6

DEALING WITH & OVERCOMING SPIRITUAL BARRIERS TO PROGRESSION

Overcoming Rejection
Confronting Fear
Overcoming Shame
Understanding the Mantle of Responsibility
Application of Right Standing

RESOURCES FOR MODULE 6

Intercession, Courts of Heaven, Timeline Healing Walking in the Mantle of Responsibility in your Stand

MODULE 7 FINISHING WELL

OCCUPYING YOUR PROMISE LAND

Change Agents
The Mountains of Influence
Your Land Shall Be Married
Preparing a Ministry for Reconciliation

www.jacquelineaniinternational.org

Note to the Stander

Welcome to The Standers Discipleship, Mentoring & Coaching Workbook. We look forward to working and supporting you in your Stand for restoration.

We know that you may be experiencing a traumatic season through the challenges in your marriage. This programme will seek to help you understand what has happened, why it has happened and how to rediscover your purpose in the Stand and your process through the Stand so that it will rebuild you to be restored back to God as a result of the Stand.

This programme will empower you while standing to:
1. Heal in your soul
2. Discover your identity in Christ
3. Position yourself to align with God for restoration
4. Preparing you for a ministry for reconciliation

The Standers Mentoring & Coaching Workbook can be used in a one to one setting or mentoring & coaching in small groups.
Thank you

Jacqueline Ani
Founder/CEO Jacqueline Ani International

MODULE 1

Introduction

About the Process

The Standers Mentorship Programme has 7 modules and can be completed in the following ways depending on your time and schedule.
1. Weekly
2. Bi weekly
3. Monthly
4. Quartely

To obtain good use of the programme you will need to complete to obtain the benefit of the programme.

The programme includes recordings for each module which you can listen to or attend the live teachings.
Each module will start with a teaching, leading into team work and then reflection to help you complete the questions and assignments in the workbook. Also a huge part of the programme will also in Bible application and reference.

Action Steps

1
Attend the teaching to the module either through recording or join the live class

2
Take part in the team work and reflective discussion and your coaching sessions if you have included it in your programme package

3
Complete the relevant section of the workbook and read the scripture references provided

Vision Board

Date _____

HEALTH

MARRIAGE

FAMILY

MINISTRY

Who is a Stander?

The process is detailed and involves following the Holy Spirit in obedience to however God wants to use the Stander to reach our spouse. Standing is also about us too, God uses it to build and develop us to align with His Will for our lives in preparation for a restored marriage. From the scripture references, we are encouraged to Stand for our loved ones without hesitation as we pray that their hearts are reunited back to God.

In the dictionary, the word stand means an attitude towards a particular issue; a position taken in an argument. A stander is someone who takes the position of standing about a certain cause, in this case it is the cause of restoration in marriage. As is implied in the word, to "stand" for your marriage means that you will pray for the restoration of your marriage and trust God in that restoration. We know that divorce is not God's will and if we ask in accordance to His will He will be faithful to hear us. Standing also includes trusting God and walking through the process with Him to restoration.

Scripture References

Ephesians 6:10-18
Matthew 24: 12-13
Galatians 5:1
1 Corinthians 16:13

Trust His Process.

What Does the Bible Say About Standing

The Bible says that there are many reasons to stand, including standing alone for the truth, standing firm in faith, and standing in worship.

Standing alone
The Bible says that there are times when people must stand alone for the truth, and that God will always be with them. For example, 1 Corinthians 15:58 says, "Therefore, my dear brothers and sisters, stand firm. Let nothing move you.

Standing firm in faith
The Bible says that people should stand firm in their faith, and that they should put on the full armor of God to do so

Standing in worship
The Bible says that people should stand in worship to show respect for God's word.

Standing with God
The Bible says that standing with God means not bowing down or giving in to anything that goes against God's will.

Standing before God
The Bible says that people will all stand before God's judgment seat, and that each person will give a personal account to God

Scripture References

Ephesians 6:10-18
1 Corinthians 15:58
1 Corinthians 16:13-14
Hebrews 13:15
Ephesians 6:14
2 Corinthians 5:10

Trust His Process.

SMART GOALS

When setting goals, make sure it follows the SMART structure.
Use the questions below to create your goals.

S	**SPECIFIC** What do I want to accomplish?	
M	**MEASURABLE** How will I know when it is accomplished?	
A	**ACHIEVABLE** How can the goal be accomplished?	
R	**RELEVANT** Does this seem worthwhile?	
T	**TIME BOUND** When can I accomplish this goal?	

NAME ★ DATE

Who is a Prodigal?

As a result they believe they are doing the right thing no matter how they hurt others in the process. They have been deceived and taken over by their own lies and the enemy of their soul.

Praying for the prodigal is a must and being healed is crucial as God works in their hearts and reconciles them back to Him.

The process for the Stander can be heavy if they have not healed and understand what it takes to stand for the prodigals restoration back to God

A person who leaves his or her responsibility to do things that God does not approve of but then feels sorry and returns home.

Prodigals can be narcissitic in behaviour as they think about themselves and make the choice to chase freedom from their responsibiities as fathers or mothers.

The choice to do this stems from what they perceive in their hearts, most times it comes from a hardened heart where they've experienced a hardness in life and they have not healed or made peace in that area of their lives.

Scripture References

Ezekiel 34:16
Jeremiah 3:13-14
Luke 15:13-24
Luke 19:10

Trust His Process.

✳ **Notes:**

✳ **Notes:**

Standers Mindset Quiz

How long have you been standing?:

- Months
- 1 to 2 years
- 3 - 5 years
- 6 - 10 years
- Over 10 years

What has challenged you most about standing? (Choose 3 responses)

- Living alone
- Lack of companionship
- Not knowing what is expected of me to be restored
- Feelings of shame and guilt
- Not knowing how to hear God
- Dating

What have you learnt through standing? (Choose 3 responses)

- Nothing
- My relationship with God has grown
- I want to discover my purpose
- Rediscovering myself
- knowing my identity in Christ
- The importance of a covenant marriage

What would you like to have achieved on completion of this programme? (Choose 2 responses)

- An increased faith in God
- My purpose and assignment
- Marriage restored
- Discerning God's voice and how He speaks to me
- A reformation in my character and attitude
- How to start a ministry

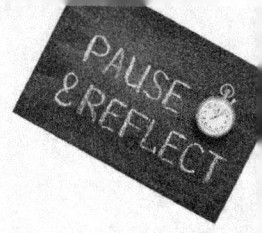

✳ Notes:

✳ **Notes:**

Monthly Planner

MONDAY	TUESDAY	WEDNESDAY	THURSDAY	FRIDAY	SATURDAY

Notes:

_____

_____

Weekly Planner

MONDAY

TUESDAY

WEDNESDAY

THURSDAY

FRIDAY

SATURDAY

SUNDAY

Old Way vs New Way

"Remember not the former things, nor consider the things of old. Behold, I am doing a new thing; now it springs forth, do you not perceive it? I will make a way in the wilderness and rivers in the desert." Isaiah 43: 18-19

THEN

What was life like for you in the past

_____
_____
_____
_____
_____
_____
_____
_____
_____
_____
_____
_____
_____

VS

NOW

What does life look like for you right now?

_____
_____
_____
_____
_____
_____
_____
_____
_____
_____
_____
_____
_____

Resources

The Standers Discipleship & Mentorship Programme comes with the following resources

Live & Recorded Teachings

You will receive a schedule with dates and times for live teaching, recordings of these teachings will also be sent to you electr

Mentoring Sessions

Coaching sessions are included in the programme. These can be booked after you've completed module 1

Workbook

The workbook must be purchased before your programme starts

For more resources check out our website jacquelineaniinternational.org

Key Symbols

The key symbols in this workbook is to help you respond to the questions authentically

Team/Group Discussions
Discussions help to understand others and their point of view, it creates an opportunity to learn from each other

Reflection Journal
Opportunity to reflect on the powerful revelations you have received. Journaling is a powerful process to capture learning

Bible Reference
Every page with this icon means there are scriptures to bring understanding from a Kingdom perspective

Kingdom Principles
Reflecting and learning the godly principle in the lesson. These principles when applied creates the desired change in us and how we are to align with God in His process in us.

Prayer Points
When listing the prayer points, always pray the scripture. This symbol is found at the end of each module.

Date: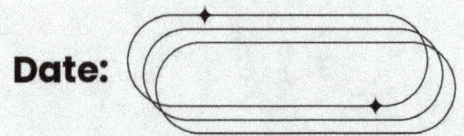

SELF- REFLECTION

1. How did I feel about this module?
_____
_____
_____
_____

2. Three principles I learnt about myself in this workshop?
✦ _____
_____
_____
✦ _____
_____
_____
✦ _____
_____

3. What principles will I apply from?:
_____
_____
_____
_____

4. How will I apply the principles I have learnt?:
_____
_____
_____
_____

5. I am grateful for:
_____
_____
_____
_____

6. Prayer points and bible scripture:
_____
_____
_____
_____

MODULE 2

Your Identity In Christ

Kingdom Principles

Ye have not chosen me, but I have chosen you, and ordained you, that ye should go and bring forth fruit, and that your fruit should remain: that whatsoever ye shall ask of the Father in my name, he may give it you. John 15:16

1. What fruit was Jesus talking about in John 15:16?
2. What does this scripture teach you?
3. What is your reflection in John 15?

What Is Identity?

Identity can mean different things to different people, and can include: Who you spend time with, The music you listen to, Where you live, and Your ethnicity.

Identity refers to our sense of who we are as individuals and as members of social groups. It also refers to our sense of how others may perceive and label us.

We develop ideas about our identities and the identities of others through our interactions with people close to us, like our family and friends, our schools and other institutions, the mass media, and our encounters with other individuals. Sometimes we don't even realize that we have these ideas because we don't remember learning them.

Personal identity refers to the unique ways that you define yourself. One person might choose to emphasize their family, religion, and interests when describing their identity. A different person might emphasize their race, neighbourhood, and job as important parts of who they are. Your personal identity consists of all the things that you believe make you, you.

This is called Cycle of Grief, you get so wrapped up in what you do that if taken away from you, you're lost

How the Bible Defines Identity

The Christian is to live with a God-defined, Jesus-centred, gospel-driven identity.

Identity is defined by God
The Bible says that everyone has an identity from God because they are made in God's image. Genesis 1:27

Identity is defined by relationship to Jesus
The Bible says that Christians have an identity in Christ, which is defined by their relationship with Jesus and what God does for them. Ephesians 1:5; **John 1:12-13**

Identity is defined by being known by God
The Bible says that believers in Christ have an identity because God knows them intimately and personally as his child. Psalm 139:1-16

Identity is defined by being made known
The Bible says that God made us who we are so that we could make known who he is.
2 **Corinthians 5:21**

Identity is defined by being hidden in Christ
The Bible says that your identity can be hidden in Christ, and that it is rooted in the revelation of who Jesus is and what he has done. **Colossians 3:3**

Cycle of Grief, Cycle of Grace

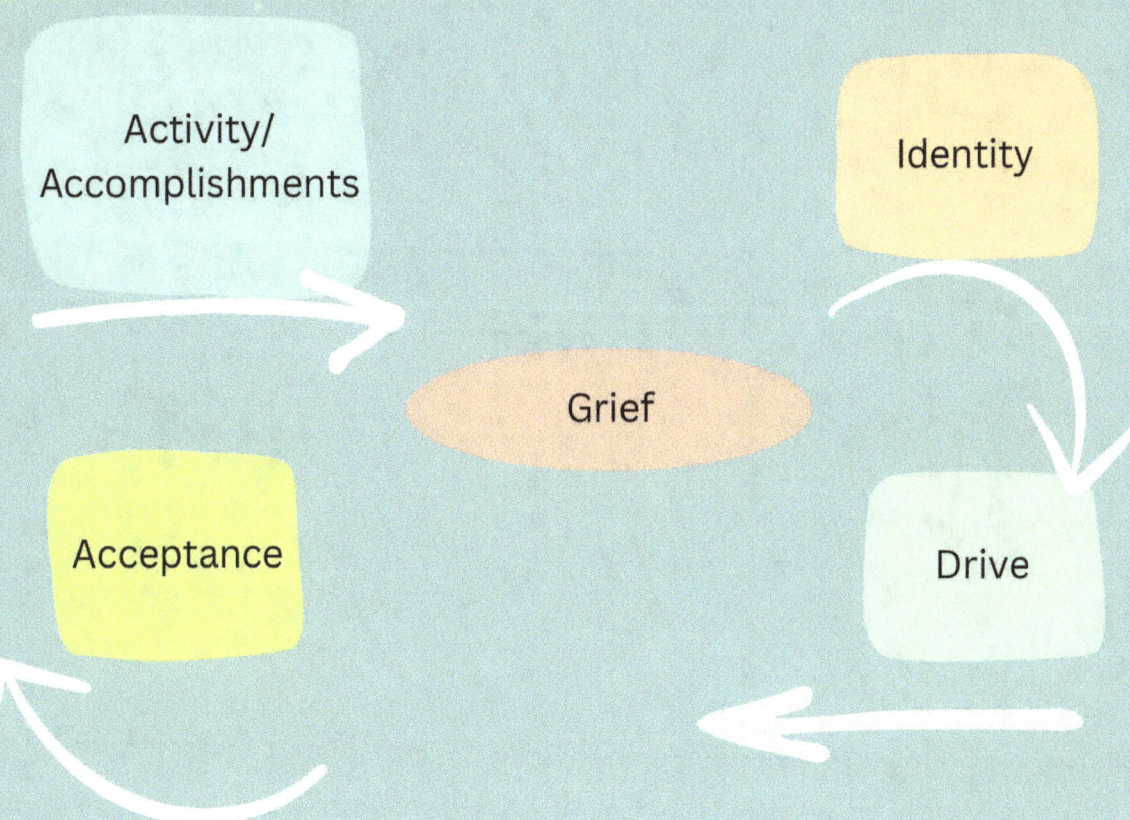

Cycle of Grief

People define themselves by their activities, their identity is defined by what they do, they obtain their drive from their activity, their drive leads them to look for acceptance from the world. This happens with celebrities who have been outdated, they need another reality fix to be re accepted by people. Take it all away they become lost. That's because the world made them what they are and they yielded to the world to accept them. When they're forced to retire, they don't know who they are anymore.

The Cycle of Grace is different.

Cycle of Grief,
Cycle of Grace

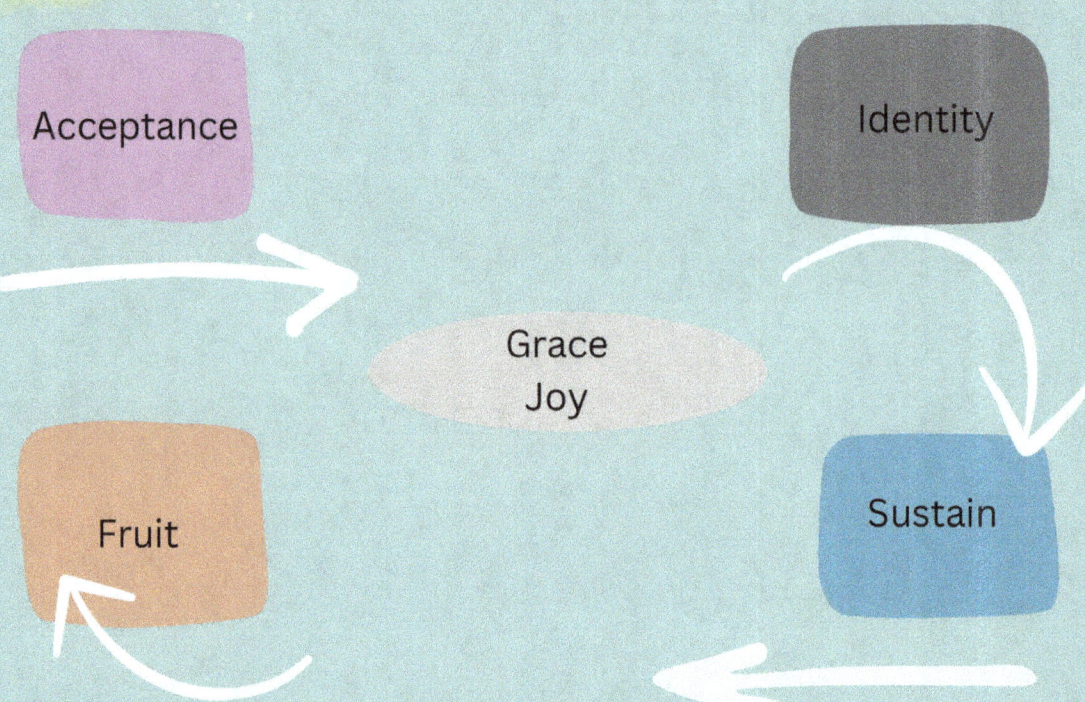

Cycle of Grace

The Cycle of Grace is all about being accepted by Jesus Christ who died on the Cross for us, that is where we get our identity from, His finshed work. Our identity doesn't come from our works, but by Grace. He sustains us, God's call on our lives is to sustain His Love in us. That word sustain is taken from John 15, if you abide in Me, I will abide in you.. He sustains us to bear fruit...

God calls you through your Stand, so that you will remain in Him and bear fruit in Him. Your Stand wasn't about you or your spouse but rather about what God wanted to use your Stand to do for the Kingdom. This means your Stand isn't about the marriage, but rather more than just the marriage, it's about Salvation, Purpose, Destiny and the Next Generation.

Using your new understanding of the Cycle of Grief and the Cycle of Grace, how has this reflected in your life? Have you been living by Grief or Grace?
- What areas in your life reflect this?
- If you have been living your life through grief, what do you need to do to change how you live through grace?

(Please use your journal to complete this section)

What is Kingdom Citizenship?

The Bible is all about a King and His Kingdom. Psalm 24:7

All nations, including kingdoms, have citizens, all nations require immigration status and the Kingdom of God is no different. Every Citizen is a naturalised citizen, we emigrated from a foreign country, a dominion of darkness.....

Think about your own country for a moment, what would you say your own citizenship is? What language do you speak? How does the government in your country operate? Are you named after the president in your country?

The Kingdom is a country of Heaven

- The governing influence of a king over his territory, impacting it with his personal will, purpose and intent
- A sovereign royal government, producing a culture, values, morals and lifestyle that reflects the king's desires and nature for his citizens
- A Kingdom is a country ruled by a king a kingdom is a nation ruled by a king it is not a religion
- In the Kingdom you own nothing we couldn't own property because in the Kingdom the king owns everything
- He allows you to use everything that's why you thank Him 24 hours a day worship never stops in the Kingdom
- In a Kingdom you never go to worship, our existence is worship that's why David says let all that has breath praise/worship Him

The Country of Heaven

- Heaven is a country it's invisible but it's a country it is the first country that existed.
- It is the original invisible country of Jehovah the name of the King is Jehovah.
- Jehovah is real
- It's more real than earth, it produced earth
- All of us used to live there, that's why deep in your psyche there is some strange awareness that you are not from Earth
- The bible says we were in Him before the foundations of the Earth
- We were inside of God's Spirit
- Therefore, Heaven is the ultimate country
- It is a supernatural country
- The word 'supernatural' was invested by us and what it means is above the natural
- Heaven is a spiritual supernatural country and you are actually a spirit, living on earth in an earth suit.
- You came from Heaven you were sent here by your government to colonize the Earth for your government

What Was Jesus' Mission?

Jesus came to earth to restore to earth:

- The Kingdom of God
- The Government of Heaven
- The Laws of Heaven
- The Values of Heaven
- The Colony of Heaven
- The Society of Heaven
- The Culture of Heaven

Thy Kingdom Come They Will Be Done......

From that time Jesus began to preach "Repent" for the Kingdom of Heaven is near (arrived)."

The original divine purpose of God was to establish a community of Heavenly Citizens on earth to extend the culture of Heaven to earth.

Jesus never said you should Go to the Kingdom, He never talked about leaving earth, but rather an experience of the Kingdom here on earth.

Therefore Kingdom is not a religion. Jesus didn't bring a religion to earth, He brought a Government.
Isaiah 7:14

Your responsibility is to learn the **constitution** of the Kingdom

Strategy to Rediscovering and Living According to the Kingdom

Jesus said seek first......He didn't say a religion, He said pursue first the Kingdom of God and His **righteousness** and EVERYTHING else shall be added to you. **Matthew 6:33**

He told us to seek a Country, not a **religion.**

Blessed are the poor in spirit for they shall see the Kingdom...

What was Abraham and Moses looking for?
- They were looking for the Kingdom but never found it.
- Jesus came after them....and pronounced Matthew 5:7; Matthew 13:45 – 46; Luke 22:29
- Jesus **conferred** - to confer is a diplomatic term used in government, when you are ordaining an ambassador in a country.
- The Bible says you are Ambassadors of Christ, you are a country.
- The devil has no right touching you, when he touches you, he is touching Heaven

How Was Kingdom Citizenship Lost?

God created the Earth and put us here. **Read Luke 19:12-27**

- To establish his Kingdom on Earth that's why it's called a far country He's telling the story of Genesis.
- The next verse says and he called his ten servants and delivered unto them 10 pounds and said unto them occupy till I come
- God sent His children to Earth to invest for Him
- When someone invest money, they want their return
- He gave them a country in a far country to receive a Kingdom and He said when I come back I want the whole place to look like this country
- And you are the ones to do it when I come back I want to see everything coming with the glory of my culture
- His citizens hated him.
- Not members, believers, but his citizens **(explain the difference)**

What Does Lost Citizenship Look Like?

The first sin was Domestic Violence
Second sin was Murder
Children being abused
Women being abused
Men being abused
Spouses abandoning their families (your experience)

We were never meant to write our own constitution

Luke 19:12 – The King (Jesus) went to far away land to bring back the Kingdom to earth and went back to Heaven. We cannot rule Earth without the Kingdom.
Luke 19:14 – They killed the King

There is a way that seems right unto man but his end is death. Proverbs 14:12

Restoration of Citizenship

- The King comes back to give us our citizenship through the Cross. **Read Luke 19: 15-18**
- The Cross is a way back but it is not the end. Religion says the Cross is the end, but it's not.
- The King brought Heaven to Earth
- He gave us a Governor (HOLY SPIRIT) so we can stay connected to Heaven
- We have permanent contact 24hrs of the day with Heaven

What Is Your Citizenship Mandate?

- We sit in Heavenly places with Jesus
- We don't live under the circumstances
- Lack of understanding your identity will keep you living under the circumstances of pain, poverty, divorce, separation, sickness etc
- To change your position and perspective
- When you recognise where you sit as a citizen, Jesus said He will give you authority to step on snakes and scorpions and none of them shall by any means hurt you. **Luke 10:19**
- You don't worry about what you will eat or drink because that's what pagans do **Matthew 6:25**
- Instead, as a citizen you are called to seek first the Kingdom of God and His Righteousness and all these things you seek will be added to you. **Matthew 6:33**

Seated In Heavenly Places

How We Ought to Pray

- Our Father, Who Art in Heaven (Country), Hallowed be Thy Name; Thy Kingdom(Country) come; Thy Will be done; on Earth as it is in Heaven (Country above). Give us this day our daily bread. And forgive us our trespasses, as we forgive those who trespass against us. And lead us not into temptation; but deliver us from evil.
- When we pray according to the Country (Kingdom) you will walk as a citizen and live like a citizen of the Kingdom
- Only pagans pray for cars, houses, clothing, food (Matthew 6:32)

What is Kingdom Purpose?

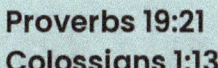

**Proverbs 19:21
Colossians 1:13**

Purpose in essence means the reason for which something has been created for or which something exists.

Purpose is very important because God created us with His Will in mind, that means God has a plan for every person He Created here on earth.

Sometimes bad things happen to good people because purpose is at work and God is Sovereign. How do you locate yourself in God's Plan for your life?

There are two types of purpose that man wants to satisfy on earth.
1. Natural Purpose
2. Divine Purpose

Natural purpose is satisfying our wants such as marriage, house, family, wealth because we want to be like others and also there is a delusion of grandeur that if we don't have these things then we have nothing.

Divine purpose is satisfying our needs, such as fulfilment, being joyful, peace and most importantly being aligned with God and what He wants for us. We locate our selves in God's plan when

- When you meet Jesus
- Accept His purpose for your life
- To be His witness
- When you become the unveiling of His Love

Locating ourselves in God's plan is to continue the work Jesus started and to do this, one must understand their assignment

How to Stand for Marriage Restoration

There has been a shift in the Kingdom, especially in marriages. Never has it been known the amount of spouses who have abandoned their marriages, families and homes because they have been deceived by the enemy that there is something better than what they already have.

The parable of the Lost Sheep in Matthew 18:10-14 teaches us how important that one sheep is for the Shepherd to leave the ninety nine to go looking for the one lost sheep.

Your process in standing is to prepare you as a vessel so that God can work through you to fulfil your assignment on earth. As a Helpmeet you in your assignment is helpful for your spouse when they return.

He prepares you to use you.

He works in you as He is working in your spouse, but there is a process to restoration and standing builds you through the process.

Proverbs 14:12 says there is a way that seems right unto man, but at the end it leads to death.

This process for the Stander is to yield to the work of God in their lives.

The process is a process of righteousness - Psalm 23:3 - He restores my soul, He leads in the path of righteousness for His Name Sake....

We are all born righteous in Christ, but not all walk in right standing and this is what God is building in you the grace to walk in right standing with Him to breakthrough.

Becoming a Vessel of Honor.

Process One - Letting Go to Let God
Letting go means exactly what it says. You've been praying for your marriage, your spouse, and now God is coming in to take full control of the situation, He is coming in to take over. You must let go of what you are holding onto, perhaps the marriage, your spouse, the memories. This process will reveal areas in your heart that is hindering you in letting go.

Process Two - Allow the Holy Spirit Expose the Issues in Your Heart
We all have issues that have built up in the deep recess of our hearts. During the time of letting go, it is important to prayerfully ask the Holy Spirit to reveal and expose issues that have been built up during the challenges in your marriage or before you got married. Issues that have been built up, keeps us from praying, spending time in His Presence. We may even have envy, jealousy, anger and anxiety that may rear it's ugly head during this period, that is why our hearts must be exposed to us.

Process Three - Renew the Understanding of Your Identity in Christ.
What does God say about you, how does He refer to you? You have to believe it. Daily meditating on the word will bring truth to the inward parts of you, being a vessel of honour means that you have to remove the lies and negative words that has been used on you, and stand on who God says you are.

Process Four - Meditate on the Word Day and Night
Develop an lifestyle where meditating on the word is part of your process. The word (Psalms and Proverbs) will renew your mind and refresh your soul, read and pray it into your being, along with that develop a time of fellowship with the Lord.

Process Five - Forgive!
You went through trauma, abuse and neglect, so it makes sense to protect yourself, however. Jesus says we must forgive 70 times 70, this means continuously forgive so that you walk in peace.

Reflect on where you have lived as a Christian, but not embracing the Kingdom Identity.
- What areas in your life do you feel you need to yield to the mission that Jesus came to Earth for?
- What was your initial understanding about marriage and where has it differed from God's original intention about marriage?
- What wounds do you think your still embracing about the fall of your marriage, how does God want you to overcome those wounds?
- Based on what you have experienced in your marriage and issues that life has presented to you, how do you think God is assigning you for His Kingdom.
- How do you see God calling you to stand for your spouse/marriage?

(Please use your journal to complete this section)

_____
_____
_____
_____
_____
_____
_____
_____
_____
_____
_____
_____
_____
_____
_____
_____

MODULE 3

Spiritual Location

Kingdom Principles

There is a season for everything,
and a time for every event under heaven
a time to be born, and a time to die;
a time to plant, and a time to uproot what was planted;
a time to kill, and a time to heal;
a time to tear down, and a time to build up;
a time to weep, and a time to laugh;
a time to mourn, and a time to dance;
a time to scatter stones, and a time to gather stones;
a time to embrace, and a time to refrain from embracing;
a time to search, and a time to give up searching;[b]
a time to keep, and a time to discard;
a time to tear, and a time to mend;
a time to be silent, and a time to speak;
a time to love, and a time to hate;
a time for war, and a time for peace. *Ecclesiastes 3:1 - 8*

1. What signs tell you that you're moving into a new season?
2. How do you prepare yourself for a new season?
3. What does this scripture teach you about your seasons of change?

Seasons of Change Autumn

Every new season requires you align with what it has to offer you. The only thing constant in life is change.

Every season you shift into has something to offer you.

"While the earth remains,
Seedtime and harvest,
Cold and heat,
Winter and summer,
And day and night
Shall not cease." *Genesis 8:22*

Like the seasons in a year; Autumn, Spring, Summer and Winter; we also go through seasons in our lives

The ability to understand what season you're in is the ability to understand how the Holy Spirit is instructing and directing you and what you must do to align with Him.

Autumn: A Season of Eating the Fruits of Your Labour.

This is the season of harvest time. It is a season of eating the fruits of your labour. All through the summer you have worked and harvested what was reaped during summer. Autumn in many cultures is a time of rejoicing.

The same applies to your spiritual life. If you dream or have a vision of Autumn, the Lord is saying that it is time to enjoy the fruit of your labour. **Leviticus 26:5**

Seasons of Change Spring

If you are in your autumn season, then you will be thinking of change, there might be some areas in your life that don't fit you or where you're heading. This period of change is crucial as it sets the tone for everything else in your life. This is the period where you should be still, confident that the new will be seen by you, meditating (praying) on the positive parts of your life and how to carry that forward into the new change. It is the time to clear out your mind and think about what you need to prepare to accommodate the change and stick with it until the change is final. Preparing an action plan is crucial during this period.

Spring: A Season of Pruning

Springtime is a season of potential. It heralds the beginning of something new. If you see a vision of spring it means that you will start to see life once again. After winter has left and the snow has melted all the seedings that had gone through death now start to come alive. It's the ultimate season of resurrection.
Songs of Solomon 2:11/12

Seasons of Change Summer

Summer: A Season of Dryness

Summer brings fruitfulness, but also a lot of hard work because the harvest is ripe. That means that now you must put your hand to the plough and bring it in.

In our spiritual lives there are times when we must work and then times when the Lord works. If you see a season of summer in the spirit, it means that now is the time for work. If you have been waiting for direction of the 'go ahead' from the Lord, seeing summer in the spirit means that now s the time to five all you have. **Proverbs 10:5**

If you're in your summer season, then you should be having a wonderful time enjoying the benefits your hard work is reaping. If you have been waiting for relationships, either business or personal (not romance related), to form this is the time to step out and form relationships that will create lasting benefits. It is important that in your summer season not to ignore your seeds of hard work that are in the ground, because you will need to harvest for your next summer season. Don't be ignorant that after summer comes winter; so don't have so much fun that you're left out in the cold.

Seasons of Change Winter

Winter: A Season of Stretching

Winter is seen mostly as negative in scripture, but also a season of rest. If you have been working hard and then
his is the period of decay, old age, death or the like. It is a time to throw out the old waiting for the dream that winter is coming then this means that a time of rest is coming.

Winter is when the fields are allowed to rest and the snow begins to fall. Although it is not always pleasant, the snow and rain feeds the soil. You cannot continually live in a season of work. You also need your seasons of Winter to step back and to allow God to do His work in your life.

Even though we know when these seasons take place in the year. The timings are different for humans (women) one woman could be in her winter season, whilst one could be in her summer season and another in her autumn season and the same for spring. You know where you are, whether you are entering into the first signs of change, or you need to do extra work, or you may be having a ball or you might be feeling stagnant. You are the leader of your life with the master plan in God's Hands.

Using what you have understood about Seasons of Change, reflect on the Seasons of Change presently happening in your life.
- Which season do you think you're in and use scripture to support this?
- Make a note of the signs or features you're experiencing in your present season.
- What do you think you have to let go of to fully operate in the new shift?

(Please use your journal to complete this section)

 Sit  Walk  Stand

Understanding Where You Are In Your Stand and Learning How to Navigate Forward

There are 3 ways to advance as a Stander in the Kingdom, referring back to our Kingdom scripture in Ecclesiastes 3:1-8, there is a time for everything under the sun and there is a process for marriage restoration. The bible says your land shall be married Isaiah 62:4, we know that the promise is restoration in your marriage, but to achieve this through God is to do the following:

- The **Sitting** Season
- The **Walking** Season
- The **Standing** Season

Part of our process as Standers is to sow after the things of the spirit and not of the flesh so that we can align with God in doing His will which also reflects in your spouse.

You are Called for such a time as this so that the marriage covenant is renewed to honour God in how He will use it for His Glory.

When you understand and apply what you must do in each stage as you advance as a Stander, you will discover why God called you out through standing for your spouse/loved one.

Scripture References
Time to Sit - Ephesians 1/2/3
Time to Walk - Ephesians 4/5
Time to Stand - Ephesians 6

Understanding Where You Are In Your Stand and Learning How to Navigate Forward

It's important to understand that everyone standing for a marriage restoration are all in different seasons and this helps to from the seasons of others, God will connect you in fellowship with people who are ahead of you in the seasons so that you learn from them and also those who you are ahead of in your season so that you can use where you are to encourage, exhort and build and in doing you move to a new season.

Another tip to identify whether you're in alignment with God as you continue in the Stand is that whatever season you're in you will see the fruits of the Spirit manifesting in and through you.

Sit in your Stand

Advancing In Your Stand Through the Sitting Season

Please Read Ephesians Chapter 2 for Reference

How do you sit when you should be standing for marriage restoration, when you should be praying, warring, praising and worship?

You want your spouse to come back immediately to continue the marriage, but it isn't as simple as we make it out to be, it is simple for God, but He wants us to go through the process and understand what is really going on spiritually. In this period, God is working on both you and your spouse, and the areas He wants us to learn about who we are in this season of the process is

1. Learn Your Identity
2. Take the Position of a Child
3. Learn the Power of Rest

We don't wrestle against flesh and blood - Ephesians 6:12, therefore the battle over your marriage is fought in the heavenly realm, you learn to love your spouse and kick the enemy out of the way, therefore your battle is not with your spouse, the battle is fought in the heavenly realm.

From our scripture reference we know that we are seated in the heavenly realms with Christ Jesus, therefore understanding your rightful place by being seated with Jesus Christ means that we know and we trust completely in God.

Sit in God's presence and see how the Lord is fighting for you.

Sit in your Stand

Advancing In Your Stand Through the Sitting Season

Learn to take a resting place at the Feet of Jesus because it is the Father's job to fight and protect us. In the sitting position we learn our identity in Christ, God is fighting for us and we don't have to strive. Sit and let god be God.

Scriptures for this Season of Sitting

- Exodus 14:14 - The Lord will fight for you an you will only need to be silent
- 2 Chronicles 20:15 - The battle doesn't belong to you, but the Lord
- Psalms 46: 9-11 - Be still and know He is God
- Psalms 37:7 - Be still and wait patiently

The sitting season is where we are sitting our heart before the Lord because there are certain things that can only be won through REST.

The main key to understanding what season you're in is through the presence of Jesus Christ and through sitting with Him, He will guide you how to go into a new season.

- What have you discovered about yourself in the sitting phase of your Stand?
- How were you managing your Stand before you realised the sitting phase?
- Explain the difference?
- What perspective can you see about the situation of your marriage and the possibility of restoration from the sitting phase?

(Please use your journal to complete this section)

Walk in your Stand

Advancing In Your Stand Through the Walking Season

The tactic of warfare is a spiritual battle and we know that God has already won the battle for us. Ephesians 6:12.

Paul says if we live in the Spirit, let us also walk in the Spirit Galatians 5:25 and to experience the Kingdom we must be like children Mark 10:15; the Kingdom of God suffers violence and the violent take it by force Matthew 11:12.

The relationship with God and the communication with Him is to know His blessings in you and how to war and take the Land (The Promise).

1. Some breakthroughs must be won, it doesn't just happen
2. The Christian life does include warfare
3. We learn the power that we possess

In the walking season, we learn the power that we as Kingdom people possess. There is power in our live and while He walks with us, He is invested in us.

Paul urges us to walk holy in a way that is suitable to your high rank given to you in your high calling. Ephesians 4:1 (The Passion Translation).

There are breakthroughs we will get when sitting and there are other breakthroughs we obtain when advancing, we have to advance to take the Land (Covenant Marriage)

Whatever revelation is revealed to you is what faith must explore and apprehend

Walk in your Stand

Advancing In Your Stand Through the Walking Season

For example, when you have a revelation that God will restore your marriage, you have to take that revelation and explore it, you must step out and apprehend it. For example in Exodus, when God gives the Israelites the Promise Land, you see how the spies walk it out, that's how we walk out the revelation of our marriage restoration.

Read Exodus 13: 17-18

The Promise Land for Standing is the restoration of your marriage, God will use the giants in the Land to teach you further before God drives them out. God can take you straight through or round the battle.

God knows what process will get you ready for battle, when He takes you straight through the battle, He knows you will win, but sometimes He has to take you round which can be longer because you have to be strengthened and trained to battle and win, just like how God prepared Gideon who was fearful of his father's household and the men of the City the Midianites to going up against them and winning the battle.

The walking season is where you have the power that God is giving you the authority of the promise. In the walking season you learn confidence, which builds strength and faith in prayer, you become stronger. The advancement brings strength and confidence and the movement brings the length of strength to survive the life when birthed.

It's in the moment you're focused because you're in a fight, your spouse is n need of deliverance. Your war is in the heavenly realm and not with your spouse.

Joshua and the Israelites had to walk through the Promise Land and walk in the Land to possess it. The Sitting season of your Stand is to understand the reality of the situation. When you're sitting you fight from a place of victory and not from a place of loss.

Walk in your Stand

Advancing In Your Stand Through the Walking Season

Understand the war is a spiritual war and:

1. The outcome is already determined.
2. We do not focus on the adversary, our focus is on God. We become victorious when we behold and embrace Jesus through the process.
3. Kow that you have the power and God has already given you victory
4. We walk with the understanfing that we fix our eyes on God

Read Ephesians 6:16

When we walk we must wear our garment for battle

The Shield of Faith - We hold up the shield of faith against the enemy's lies
The Helmet of Salvation - We wear the helmet of salvation to protect our mind and the negative words that would pierce our soul.
The Sword of the Spirit - The sword of the spirit is the Word of God and we cannot walk through without understanding what the word says so that when the attack comes to settle, we use the word to uproot the lies from our mind.

Wars are won by relying on the promises of God

Read 1 Timothy 1:18

Remember the prophecies made about you, so that you may wage a good warfare, by fightng the good fight of faith.

God is using the process to produce a beautiful war.

Walk in your Stand

Advancing In Your Stand Through the Walking Season

The Promises of God for your life have already been spoken and determined, if you reject them, your hearts will be destroyed.

Scriptures for this Season of Walking

- Proverbs 18:21 - Speak your promises out loud, don't take the promises and sit and do nothing.
- Hebrews 11:3 - It must be done by faith
- Mark 11:23 - What are you saying to the mountain you're facing?
- 2 Corinthians 4:13 - God requires us to partner with our belief when we speak it.
- Psalm 103:20 - Bless the Lord, the angels obey the voice of His Word. Lose angels to fight on your behalf.
- Genesis 28:18 - Jacob put a stone at Bethel and anointed the stones with oil.
- Joshua 4:3/6 - Put things up in your life as a reminder of the promise.
- 1 Samuel 7:12 - David put a stone and named the place Ebenezer

- What have you learn about yourself in the walking season of your Stand?
- How has walking in your stand equipped you for Standing?
- What areas of your life needed to be strengthened so that you can stand in agreement with God to take back the Promise of Marriage Restoration?
- What is the Holy Spirit exposing to you about the condition of your heart relating to your spouse in your walking season?

(Please use your journal to complete this section)

Stand in your Stand

Advancing In Your Stand Through the Standing Season

Paul instructs us to stand firm, which is fighting from a different position to the walking season. In this season God equips us to Stand and to not cave in.

Read Ephesians 6:11-14

After you've done everything to stand, Stand!

With the weight of issues coming against you, with everything that may want to set you back, this is the phase that you don't lose ground, you don't give up. You may not be advancing, but what you're doing is that you're not losing ground, in this phase you learn the supernatural ability to stand firm.

Read Hebrews 6:11-15

Patiently enduring to obtain the promise, but we also need to have the ability to stand firm like Abraham.

Read 2nd Corinthians 4:8-9

Everything you've learnt in the Sitting and Walking phase is to be applied in the Standing phase. You can take the blows, but you're not to give up on your stand

Stand in your Stand

Advancing In Your Stand Through the Standing Season

There are moments we have to be okay for not winning.

Read Galatians 6:9

You have permission to feel the emotions, but you must not give up.

Read 2 Corinthians 12:9

The Standing period presents moments of trials and tests and we are called to stand firm in the trial and not run from it.

Read James 1:2-4

Our faith being tested produces patience, so that patience can have it's perfect work that we may be courageous.

Read 2 Peter 1:3

Read Psalm 100:4

The Standing phase produces endurability as we stand in thanksgiving, joy and praise. As we faithfully stand, God shifts our perspective on how we see trials and tests and shifts us from what is going on or what will distract.

Read 1 Peter 1: 6-7

Stand in your Stand

Advancing In Your Stand Through the Standing Season

Read 1 Peter 1: 6-7

Your faith through this is been proved to be genuine, resulting in praise, glory and honour when Jesus is revealed, therefore the test has a purpose.

Why is it important that God proves the genuineness of our faith?

Answer - It pleases God.

We are not to give up because there is Glory at the end of the Test.

4 Types of Biblical Test

Endurance /Patient Test (Abraham)
Radical Obedience Test (Abraham)
Opposition to the Promise Test (Caleb & Joshua)
Temptation of Sin Test (Jesus)

- What have you learn about yourself in the standing season of your Stand?
- How has standing in your stand equipped you for restoration?
- What areas of your life needed to be strengthened so that you can stand in agreement with God to take back the Promise of Marriage Restoration?
- What is the Holy Spirit exposing to you about the condition of your heart relating to your marriage in your standing season?
- Take the Love Language Personality Test https://blossomup.co/
- From your results, what do you understand about your Love Language

(Please use your journal to complete this section)

Healing Your Soul

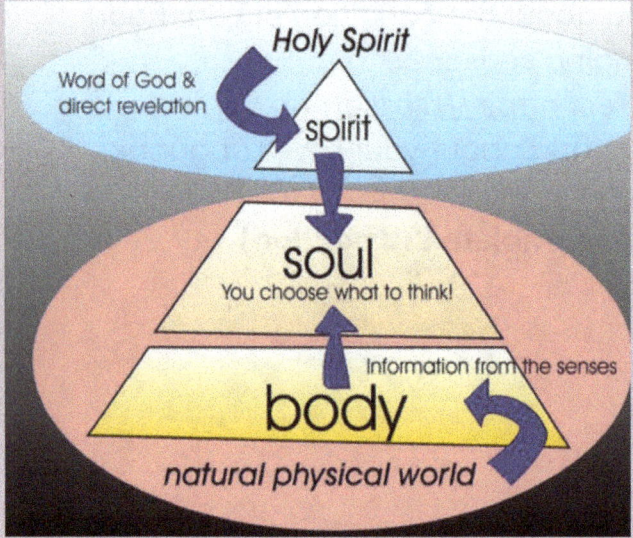

Man is triune in nature, he has a spirit, a soul and a body

Read Genesis 1:26 – 27

We are triune beings, made in the image of God (with HIS Likeness). We are spirits, we have a soul made up of our mind, will and emotions, and we live in a body.

Our spirit is number 1 on the totem pole so to speak in relation to our spirit, soul and body.

When people think about themselves, they look at what they can see with their natural eyes.

When they look in the mirror and see their physical body, they believe that is WHO they are.

There is a distinct difference between our spirit, soul and body and it is important to understand each part and how they operate.

The Godhead is a 3 Part Being
- God the Father
- God the Son
- God the Holy Spirit

Healing Your Soul

Man is triune in nature, he has a spirit, a soul and a body

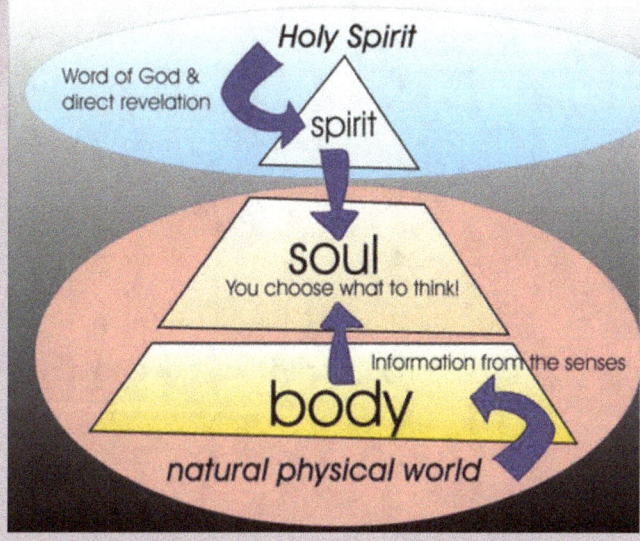

Read 1 Thessalonians 5:23

In HIS Image
- You are a spirit (spirit man) - made completely perfect through salvation.
- You have a soul (mind, will, emotions)
- You live in a body (your house)

1. Your Spirit Definition
The spirit comes from God and is knit to the cells of mankind. This is the part of mankind that after repentance and conversion is made completely new.

Your Spirit is made completely NEW at conversion.(Repentance & Our Faith in Jesus).
2 Corinthians 5:17

2. Your Soul Definition
The soul is comprised of the mind, will and emotions.

The GATES to the soul are our imagination, conscience, memory, reason and affections.

Our soul is transformed and changed over time by yielding to the Holy Spirit.
Romans 12:2; 2 Corinthians 10:5; Galatians 5:16-24; 1 Peter 2:11

Healing Your Soul

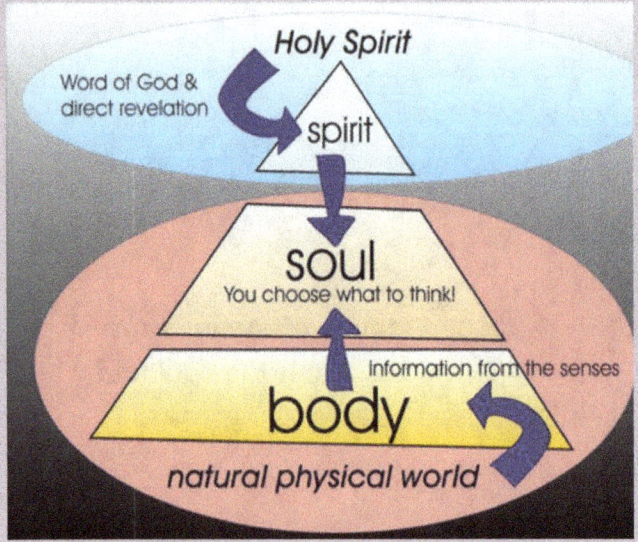

Man is triune in nature, he has a spirit, a soul and a body

Jesus' Spirit & Soul
"...the ruler of this world is coming, and he has NOTHING in Me." John 14:30

Jesus was sinless & therefore His soul was uncontaminated **1 Peter 2:22; Hebrews 4:15; 1 John 3:5**

The enemy was furious and terrified that he couldn't find anything to hook his claws into Jesus.
He couldn't tempt Jesus in the wilderness during those 40 days nor could he deceive Jesus. Jesus was pure...spirit, soul and body.

Reference - Matthew 4 & Luke 4. There are two different accounts of the same story.

There is a story about Jesus coming to a man who lived among the tombs who had a legion of demons. These demons spoke through the man to Jesus and said basically that they couldn't find anything in common with Jesus. That meant they could not hurt Jesus or attach to Jesus. Reference **Matthew 8; Mark 5 and Luke 8**. There are three different accounts of "Legion" in the Bible.

Healing Your Soul

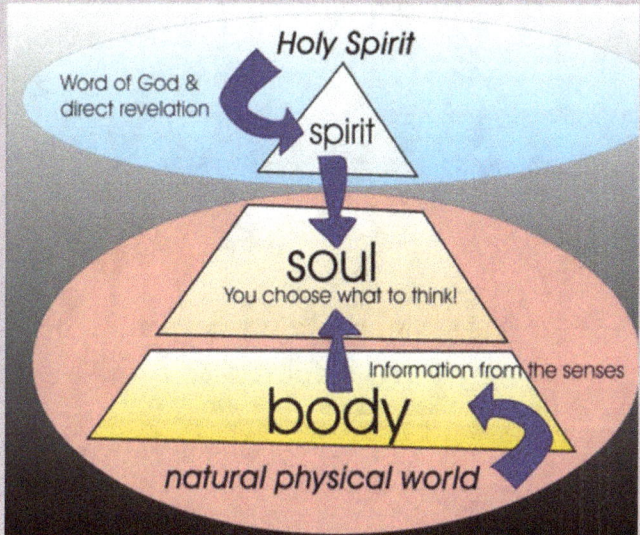

Man is triune in nature, he has a spirit, a soul and a body

What Impacts Our Soul

- Our DNA or actions of our forefathers
- Words Spoken Over Us/Word Cursing/Vows
- Rejection/Abandonment
- Unwantedness
- Bullying
- Abuse
- Sinning/Being Sinned Against
- Sexual Sin/Molestation/Rape/Incest
- Trauma
- Things Entering through the Eye/Ear Gate:
- Media/Music/Verbal Abuse/Porn/Violence

Think about the list above *are there any other issues you can think of that isn't on the list?*

Healing Your Soul

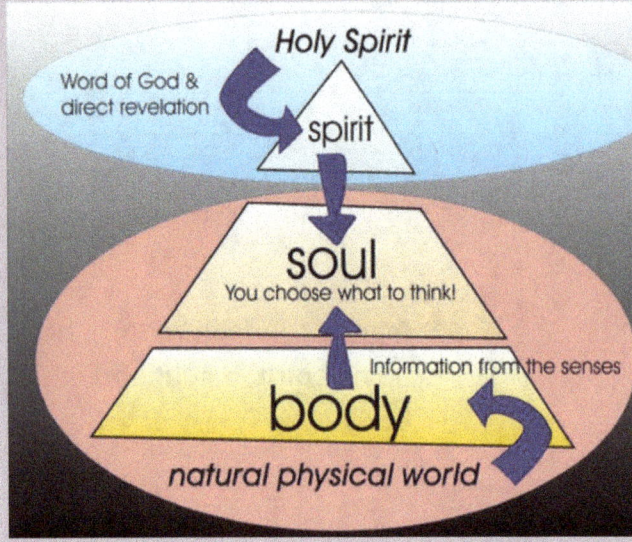

Man is triune in nature, he has a spirit, a soul and a body

When we sin, we know that we are to go to Jesus and repent for our sins. However, generational iniquities, our sins and trauma injure our soul. The enemy cannot touch our spirit man; however, he can get to our soul and our body if he can find something to latch onto. Since we are born into sin, our souls normally have things attached to them even at birth. They are attached to the DNA, the mind, will and emotions. Various issues can be passed along through our bloodlines.

When we received Jesus our spirit man became born again and we came under God the Father (The Creator). Our spirit cannot be touched by the enemy because Christ's spirit comes inside of us to live in us. We are the temple (the house) of the Holy Spirit...our spirit man.

Any intruders attached to the spirit have to vacate at the time of salvation. If they have a legal right, they can remain in our soul as believers. We can have portions of our soul that are healthy and portions of our soul that are unhealthy.
The soul of a non-believer may have even more fracture or wounded parts. Sometimes soul fractures are label as personality defects or normal. A nonbeliever may think their issues are normal.

Healing Your Soul

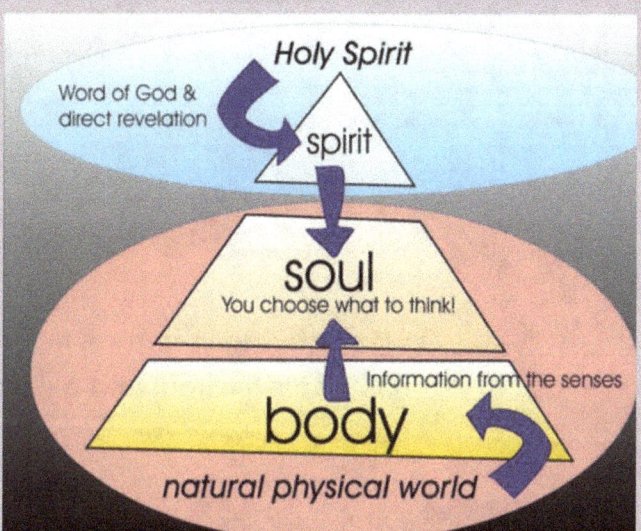

Man is triune in nature, he has a spirit, a soul and a body

1. How early can a soul wound occur in a person's life? *Read Matthew 12:44-46*

_____
_____
_____
_____
_____

2. Why spend so much time talking about the soul?

_____
_____
_____
_____
_____

Healing Your Soul

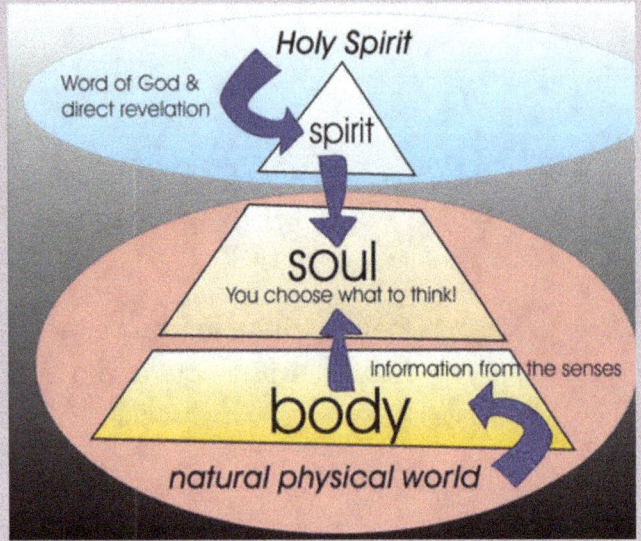

Man is triune in nature, he has a spirit, a soul and a body

Bruised Fruit is an example used to show what happens to our souls when they are wounded.

This is what the condition of our soul with wounds looks like verses a cleansed soul

Healing Your Soul

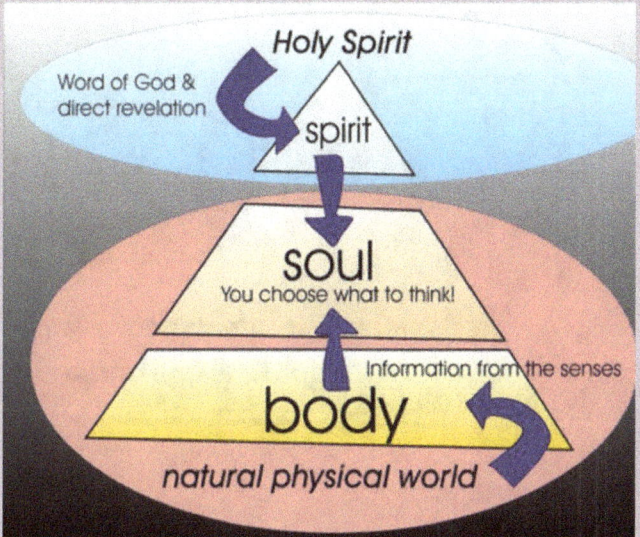

Man is triune in nature, he has a spirit, a soul and a body

Imagine a garbage can. The garbage represents generational/sin/traumas...soul wounds.
Just like a garbage can left unattended, the flies and maggots begin to swarm the trash of rotten food and trash.
The flies are attracted to the trash in the trash can.

When our souls are left unattended, the enemy is attracted to the hurts, pains of life, sin that is left unattended. One of the reasons we seek to do inner healing PRIOR to deliverance is to clear out as much of the bruised and rotting pieces as possible. If you simply cast the spirits out and do not deal with the root cause, the soul wound, there is a potential for the spirits to return and try to make the situation worse. One of the reasons traditional deliverance leaves people still struggling at times is the lack of dealing with the soul wounds that the demonic spirits are feasting on inside the person.

Wounds on the Soul Occur Due to:

- Abandonment
- Abuse
- Assault
- Betrayal
- Bullying
- Being Unwanted by Parent/Different Gender
- Generational Sins
- Neglect
- Trauma
- Racism

Healing Your Soul

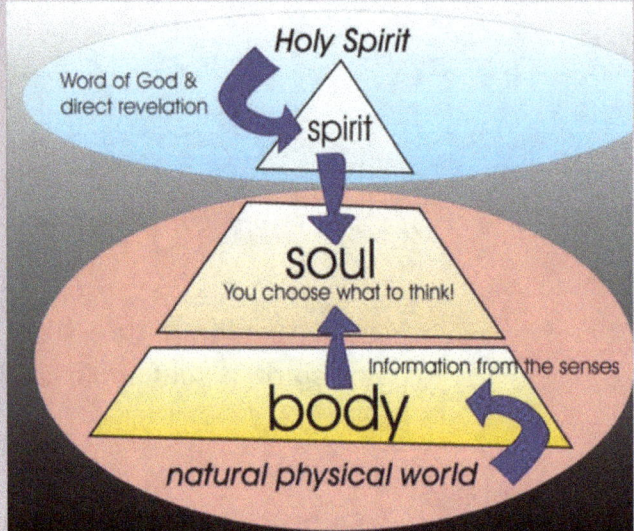

Man is triune in nature, he has a spirit, a soul and a body

The Soul Train Structure
- **Our bodies are connected to our souls.**
- **Our souls are connected to our spirit.**
- **Our spirit is connected to the Spirit of God.**

See how they connect yet are different. Our soul cannot receive forgiveness of sins, it is our spirit that receives forgiveness of sins. Our soul connects to our spirit that enables us to renew our mind.

Our emotions are a temperature gauge to help us know the condition of our soul.

All of these are part of WHO God is.

Remember...you ARE a spirit and you have a soul; both of these we cannot see with the natural eye and they are eternal.

Healing Your Soul

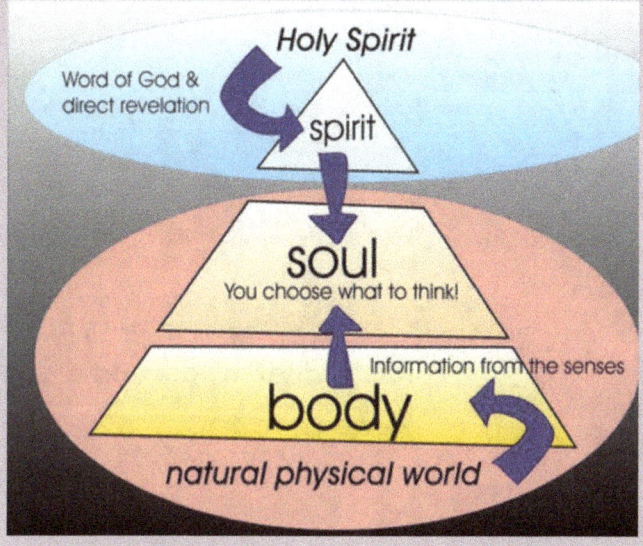

Man is triune in nature, he has a spirit, a soul and a body

3. Our Body Definition
The body is our physical shell that houses our spirit and soul. The physical body will return to the earth.
It is known as the part of humanity that touches the material world through our FIVE SENSES:

Sight, Smell, Hearing, Tasting, and Touching
(These 5 mirror the Spiritual Senses)

Read 3 John 2 Amplified Version

We know that our body houses our spirit and soul. They are intertwined, yet can be divided!

Whatever happens in our soul manifests in our body...Scientific research is catching up with the Bible.

What about when people pray for a body to be healed and nothing happens? Each case is unique and individual but many times when you get the soul healed, the body is healed. If the soul is sick, the body is sick. **Read Hebrews 4:12**

Healing Your Soul

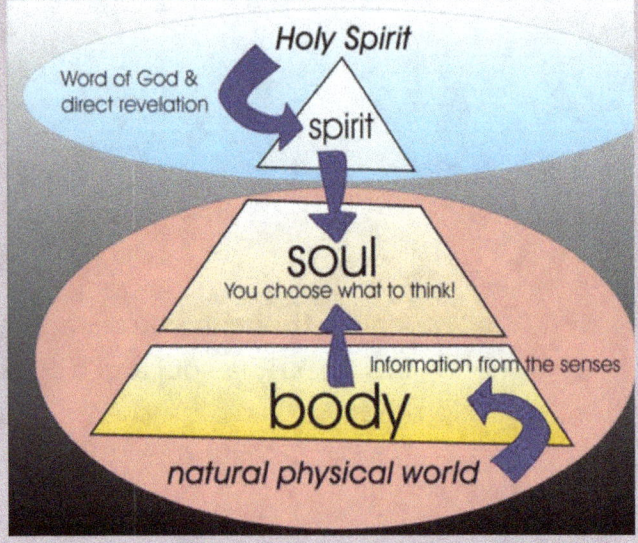

Man is triune in nature, he has a spirit, a soul and a body

Function of the Spirit:
Our spirit is the core part to connect with the spiritual realm. Those who worship God MUST worship Him in SPIRIT & TRUTH (John 4:24). Non-believers can connect to the spirit realm as well, but through the wrong source.

Function of the Body:
The body is the easiest to understand. It is used to interact with the physical world and through our five senses.

Function of the Soul
The soul is WHO we are. Our soul is made up of our mind, will and emotions. The function is to EXPRESS GOD.

Our soul is divided into the Mind, Will and Emotions

Our Mind:
The main battlefield is in our mind. Our mind and how we think moves to how we feel in our emotions and it also affect our choices.

The enemy of our souls is after destroying the very thing that God loves the most. Me & You.

Healing Your Soul

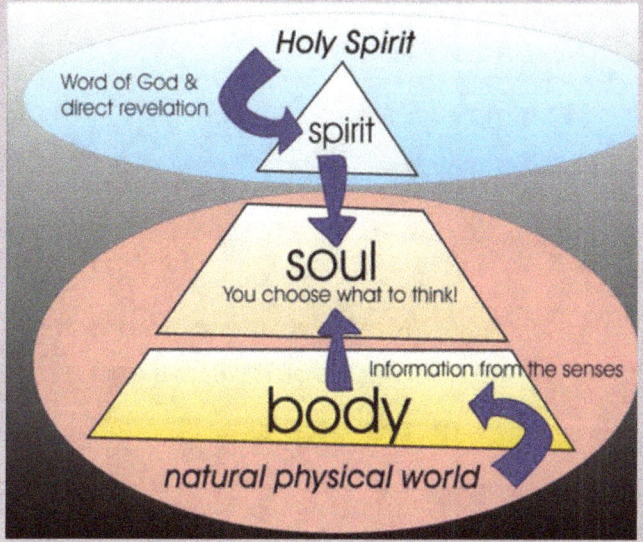

Man is triune in nature, he has a spirit, a soul and a body

Our Will
Is either submitted to Jesus or to Satan.

It is one or the other. When we say, "I will" or "I will not" we are exercising the beautiful free gift to CHOOSE that God granted only to human beings. We want people to love us by their own FREE WILL! God wants relationship by someone's own FREE WILL. The gift to CHOOSE.

Our Emotions:
Our emotions are our gage to connect with what is really going on in our soul. We use a thermometer to take our body temperature and we know that if that thermometer reads above a certain mark it is a warning to pay attention that something is not right in our bodies and needs immediate attention.

Our emotions are the thermometer of our soul. There are healthy emotions and there are unhealthy emotions. When unhealthy emotions arise and left unchecked bad fruit is developed.

Healing Your Soul

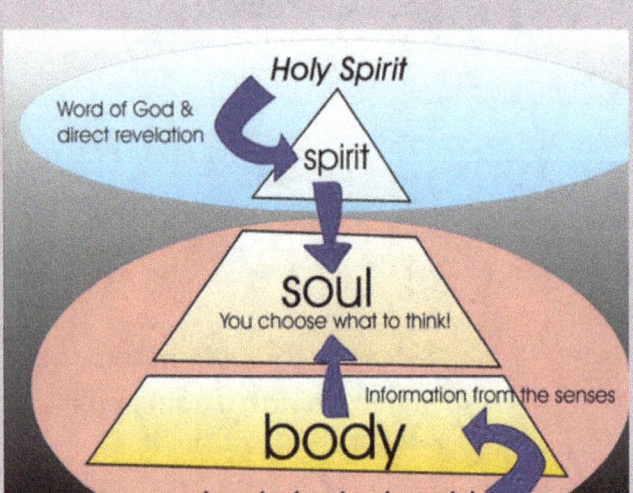

Man is triune in nature, he has a spirit, a soul and a body

WHAT ARE DEMONS?

Demons are fallen angels. When Lucifer rebelled, 1/3 of the angels followed him. They offered their allegiance to the devil. **Revelations 12:9**

Kinds of Demons
- Rulers
- Authorities
- Cosmic Powers
- Spiritual Forces of Evil in Heavenly Places
  Ephesians 6:13

It is good to note that none of these entities are more powerful than God. They are created beings, nor the Creator. God sits at the very top and there are none more powerful than God. All demons and Satan are subject to God and the name of Jesus. Therefore, we are not to walk in fear or timidity with the demonic.

Demons possess the great power of angels (**Romans 8:38; 1 Corinthians 15:24**), greater than humans but far less than their Creator. They have the power to carry out the following actions:

Healing Your Soul

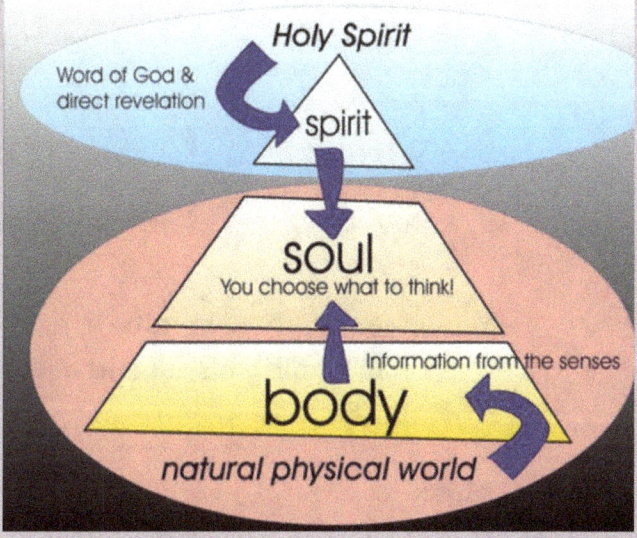

Man is triune in nature, he has a spirit, a soul and a body

- Indwell humans and animals **(Mark 5:1-16)**
- Physically afflict people **(Mark 9:17, 22)**
- Terrorize humans **(1 Samuel 16:14-15; 18:10; 19:9; Acts 19:13-16; 2 Corinthians 12:7)**
- Initiate false worship **(1 Corinthians 10:20-21)**
- Promote false doctrines **(1 Timothy 4:1)**
- Perform false signs and wonders **(2 Thessalonians 2:9; Revelation 16:13-14)**
- Deceive prophets **(1 Kings 22:19-23)**
- Encourage idolatry **(Deuteronomy 32:17; Psalm 106:37)**
- Engineer death **(Judges 9:23, 56-57)**

Healing Your Soul

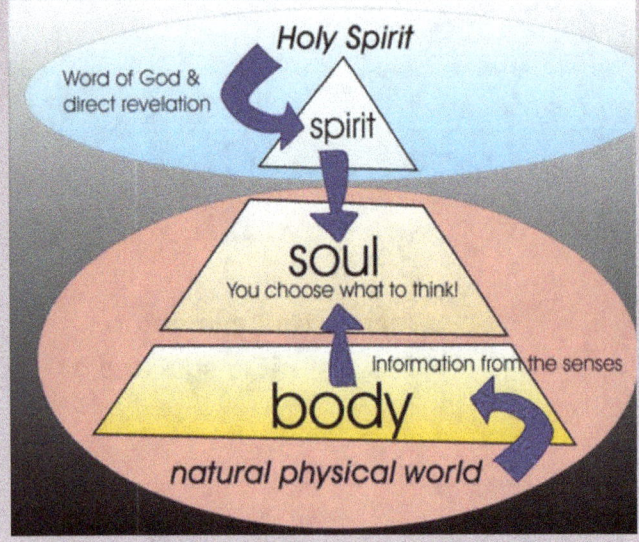

Man is triune in nature, he has a spirit, a soul and a body

THE TUG OF WAR WITH DELIVERANCE.
Can a Christian have a Demon Operating In Them?

_____
_____
_____
_____
_____
_____
_____
_____

Having demons does NOT call a believer's salvation into question. Demons can hinder a person but they cannot take away a person's salvation.

Healing Your Soul

Man is triune in nature, he has a spirit, a soul and a body

Demons come in families or are grouped together.
Rejection
is the #1 spirit and is best friends with lust and perversion. This is a popular spirit in many people's lives opens the door to many other spirits to come in.

Anger:
Group may include hatred, self-hatred, rage, abuse

Lust:
Group may include fantasy lust, sexual perversion, fornication, adultery, immorality, incest, rape, homosexuality, pornography, compulsive masturbation.

Bitterness:
Group may include unforgiveness, resentment, jealousy, envy (manifested in the body through cancer)

Shame: best friends with insecurity and fear
Group may include low self-esteem, low self-worth, self-sabotage, self-hatred, self-rejection

Healing Your Soul

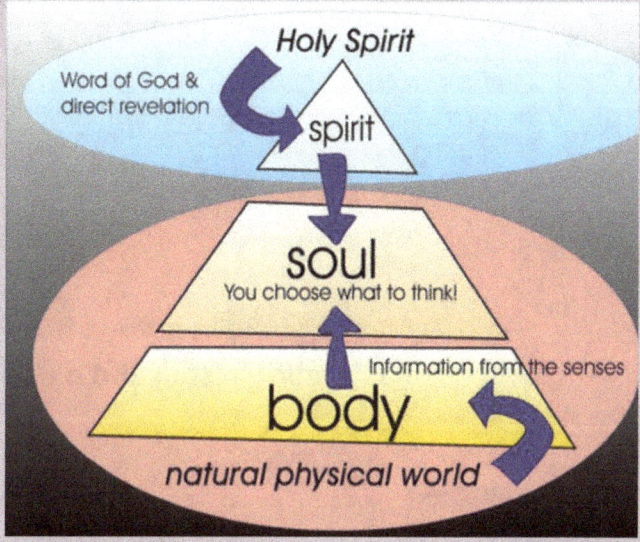

Man is triune in nature, he has a spirit, a soul and a body

STRONG DEMONS:
Freemasonry & Occult Demons (in most bloodlines) are very legalistic.
Catholicism has a lot of witchcraft demons
False Religions
Jezebel/Ahab Spirits
Marine Spirits
Leviathan

IDOLATRY IS A STRONG DEMON
When helping those that seem stuck or get minimal to no breakthrough check for idols!!

The devil will not budge where there is legal ground. One place I am learning to check is for idols. The person can claim to love Jesus all day and be spirit filled, yet they have erected an idol in their lives.
Common IDOLS are...

Healing Your Soul

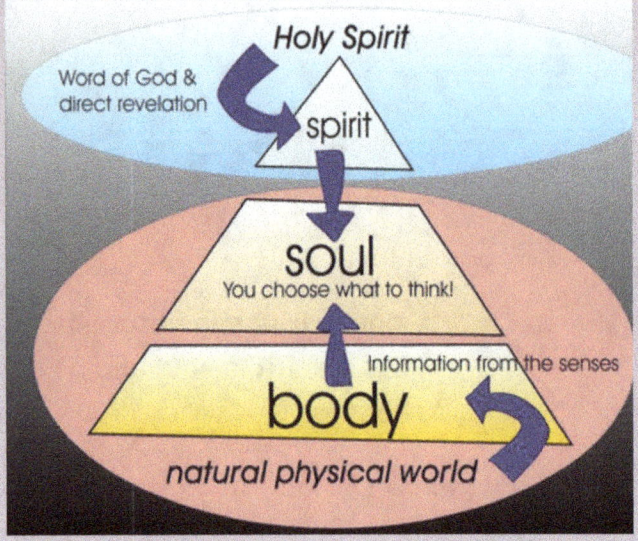

Man is triune in nature, he has a spirit, a soul and a body

Self (self-pity, pride, self-reliance instead of God reliance, victim mentality)
These demons often go undetected and the person thinks they are good, but behind the scenes are **high level demons of Leviathan and often Jezebel.**

Self-pity and the victim demon partner with Jezebel spirits to make the person manipulative. **They gain power by making the person very self-focused and pitiful or a martyr. It feeds off attention the person gets for being a victim or in bad place.** Therefore, when you try to help, the demon will only let you get so far. The person gains something from being broken.

Some say they want to be free yet subconsciously feed off being broken. You cannot help people who do not want to be free or are not ready for freedom. Some parts (alters) do not want to be free while the core person does.

Success (pride in what they can do or figure out on their own)
Instead of being God reliant, they are self-reliant. Pride will buck you in deliverance.

There is part of the person that thinks they don't need help though they came to see you. Pride keeps them in bondage and since they appear successful, their agreement with pride may cause you problems.

Healing Your Soul

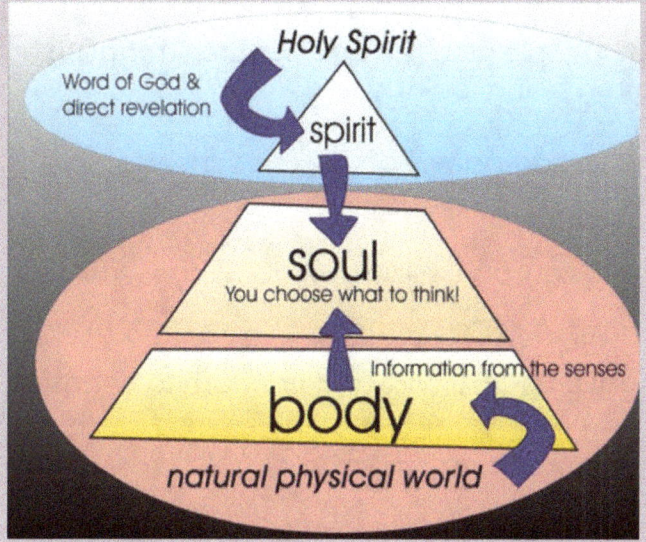

Man is triune in nature, he has a spirit, a soul and a body

People:
Ministers, Ministry, Friend, Spouse, Child

They created an idol out of a person. That person will talk about the other person A LOT

Function of Demons

- Addiction – demons love bondage – many people who are addicts are struggling with STRONG demons. The main demon often being idolatry.

- Brokenness – they love to break things...lives, marriages, homes, relationships, churches, etc.

- Confusion – identity confusion, gender confusion, confusion of WHO God is, WHAT God says.

- Control – impose their will on host. Jesus gave us FREE WILL and freedom to choose.

- Cycles of Pain – they love pain and suffering.

- Death – comes to kill, steal and destroy and pushes people to cut, suicide, binging and recklessness

- Deception – The devil is a LIE J LOL

- Destruction – demons hate people because Jesus loves them. Demons want to hurt what the Father loves.

- Discouragement/Depression – note: not all depression is demonic. Some depression can be biological.

- Division/Discord – Pride is present when there is discord. Where strife is there is every evil work.

- Doubt – Eve was the first example where doubt was presented to her about what God said.

- Embarrassment – embarrassment and shame are tools to ensnare people and keep them trapped.

Function of Demons

- Fear – One of the Chief Spirits in the demonic kingdom. Fear is the Faith in the wrong kingdom.

- Gossip/Slander – traps many "Christians" with this spreading to hurt another's reputation.

- Insecurity/Inferiority – this is a hidden form of pride.

- Jealousy – linked to a spirit of murder.

- Lust – also rooted in selfishness. Self-gratification rather than love which is selfless. Lust opens the door to addiction.

- Making things worse – problems worsen through the function of demons

- Murder – take life, kill dreams, kill hope, kill reputations.

- Perversion – twist God's word which is Truth. Sexual twisting and authors of false doctrines and cults.

- Pride – arrogance and pride is what got the devil booted out of heaven. Pride is elevating our opinion above God's. Pride is the root of insecurity.

- Rejection – Opens doors to spirits of shame, self-hatred, rejection of others, lust, perversion. Lust and rejection work together. Lust provides false love.

- Strife – a very evil spirit. Angry or bitter disagreement over fundamental issues; conflict

- Sickness – sickness and disease are results of the fall of man. Demons bring sickness and infirmities.

- Trauma – love to cause trauma and situations that cause trauma. Trauma brings infirmity.

- What issues growing up has impacted your soul that may still be affecting you in your Stand and Restoration?
- What measures have you taken to address these issues?
- Have these issues been resolved?
- Have you forgiven your spouse for their behaviour towards you in the marriage?
- If not, what do you think is keeping you in an unforgiven state towards them?
- Have you forgiven your behavior towards your spouse that contributed to the separation/divorce?
- How is your renewed state reflected in your behaviour and your life?
- Where are you in your *emotions, will and thoughts* regarding your Stand?

(Please use your journal to complete this section)

MODULE 4

Identifying & Possessing Your Gift for Purpose

Kingdom Principles

A gift opens the way and ushers the giver into the presence of the great Proverbs 18:16

1. Make a list of the gifts you possess?
2. How have you used your gifts to create opportunities in your sphere of environment?
3. What do you possess in your home that you have overlooked that may be of sale value? 2 Kings 4:1-7

The Three Categories of Gifts

Each of you should use whatever gift you have received to serve others, as faithful stewards of God's grace in its various forms.
1 Peter 4:10

We have different gifts, according to the grace given to each of us. If your gift is prophesying, then prophesy in accordance with your faith; if it is serving, then serve; if it is teaching, then teach; if it is to encourage, then give encouragement; if it is giving, then give generously; if it is to lead, do it diligently; if it is to show mercy, do it cheerfully.
Romans 12:6-8

Now about the gifts of the Spirit, brothers and sisters, I do not want you to be uninformed. You know that when you were pagans, somehow or other you were influenced and led astray to mute idols. Therefore I want you to know that no one who is speaking by the Spirit of God says, "Jesus be cursed," and no one can say, "Jesus is Lord," except by the Holy Spirit.
There are different kinds of gifts, but the same Spirit distributes them. There are different kinds of service, but the same Lord. There are different kinds of working, but in all of them and in everyone it is the same God at work.
Now to each one the manifestation of the Spirit is given for the common good. To one there is given through the Spirit a message of wisdom, to another a message of knowledge by means of the same Spirit, to another faith by the same Spirit, to another gifts of healing by that one Spirit, to another miraculous powers, to another prophecy, to another distinguishing between spirits, to another speaking in different kinds of tongues, and to still another the interpretation of tongues. All these are the work of one and the same Spirit, and he distributes them to each one, just as he determines.
1 Corinthians 1-11

The Manifestation Gifts

Pages 172-176

The Manifestion Gifts are found in 1 Corinthians 12: 7-10 READ.

There are 9 gifts listed in this category:

Word of Wisdom
a revelation of wisdom beyond natural human wisdom that enables a person to know what to do or say

Word of Knowledge
a revelation of the information for a person, group, or situation that could not have been known by any natural means

Faith
the kind of wonder-working faith that moves mountains and waits expectantly for results

Gifts of Healing
the many different ways and varieties of degrees in which God manifests healing

Working Miracles
the demonstration of the power and action of God that goes beyond natural laws

Prophecy
an anointed proclamation of God through an individual to encourage, exhort or comfort

Discerning of spirits
a person's ability to perceive what type of spirits is in operation in a given situation

Various kinds of tongues
the language given to the believer by the Holy Spirit but not learned or understood by the speaker

Interpretation of tongues
the supernatural ability to express the content of what has been spoken in tongues

The Ministry Gifts

The Ministry Gifts are found in Ephesians 4:11 READ

There are 5 gifts listed in this category:

The Evangelist

The Pastor

The Teacher

The Motivational Gifts

The Motivational Gifts are found in Romans 12:6-8. These are the gifts we possess, they are gifts that God has built into us, made part of us to be used for the benefit of others and for His glory. They are the gifts that shape our personalities.

There are 7 gifts listed in this category;

One who clearly perceives the will of God
Perceiver

One who loves to serve others
Server

One who loves to research and communicate truth
Teacher

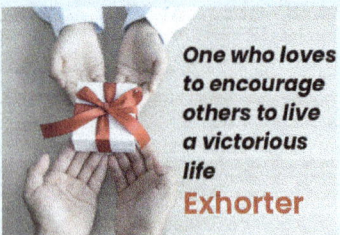
One who loves to encourage others to live a victorious life
Exhorter

One who loves to give time, talent and energy to benefit others
Giver

One who loves to organise, lead and direct
Administrator

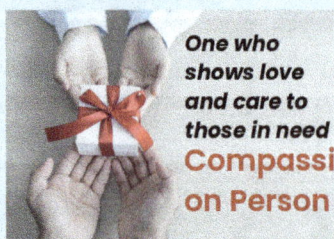
One who shows love and care to those in need
Compassion Person

Take the Survey — Page 177

Adding Value to the Motivational Gifts

Please complete the spiritual and motivational surveys and save your answers for your group discussions.

Once you have identified what your motivational gifts are, then you can start adding value to improve the gift, for example if you have scored high in teaching, but you may not have any technique or knowledge, what can you do to enhance your skills and technique in the gift so that you are fruitful in your calling and assignment. Remember your gifts are to bless others, the Light of Christ in you is to bless His people and He is using you as a vessel to do this. Also as a Stander you are called to fulfil God's mandate on your life and this also entails knowing and using you gifts.

The importance of using our motivational gifts for the glory of God is the only way you will find fulfilment, these gifts are the motivational force for our lives, and unless they are channelled properly, you cannot help but feel frustrated. However, once discovered, you have also discovered a tremendous potential for happiness.

Our Gift Was Built Into Us When God Formed Us

Our giftedness was not an afterthought. It was part of God's plan to shape us for our role in the building of His Kingdom.

One of the most beautiful creation passages in the Old Testament is found in Psalm 139:13-16 Read!

What a magnificent expression of the design and development of the child in the womb. God uses what scientists now call DNA in the process.

Every detail of our physical being is programmed by DNA. It's intricacies far outweigh the most sophisticated computer system on the market today, the colour of your hair was pre programmed by your DNA. The shape of your nose, your height, your body frame, all your physical characteristics were determined at that moment of conception.

If God has so precisely planned for the development of your physical body which is eventually subject to degeneration and death, how much more has He planned for your giftedness. We believe that our motivational gifts are given to us at conception and that just as DNA eventually brings forth our physical characteristics, so our motivational gifts bring forth the interest, abilities, enthusiasms and actions that make us effective members of the Body of Christ.

We are not to neglect our gift 1 Timothy 4:14 Read

Our Gift Colours All that We See

A Perceiver	A Server
A Teacher	An Exhorter
A Giver	An Administrator

A Compassion Person

And each person will wonder why others don't see things the way they see them
What we are is God's gift to us;
What we make of our lives is our gift to God.

How Does Our Gift Colour What We See?

From a study, here is the breakdown of people with the different gifts

Gift	%
Perceiver	12%
Server	17%
Teacher	6%
Exhorter	16%
Giver	6%
Administrator	13%
Compassion Person	30%

Why do you think God gives some gifts more frequently than others?

Each Gift Is of Equal Value

Gift	Definition	Need Met	Function
Perceiver	Declares the Will of God	Spiritual	Keeps Us Concentrated on Spiritual Things
Server	Renders Practical Service	Practical	Keeps the Work of the Ministry Moving
Teacher	Researches and Teaches the Bible	Mental	Keeps Us Studying and Learning
Exhorter	Encourages Personal Progress	Psychological	Keeps Us Applying Spiritual Truth
Giver	Shares Material Assistance	Material	Keeps Specific Needs Provided For
Administrator	Gives Leadership and Direction	Functional	Keeps Us Organised and Increases Our Vision
Compassion Person	Provides Personal and Emotional Support	Emotional	Keeps Us in the Right Attitudes and Relationships

Interpreting Your Gift Survey Results

The Gift You Function in All the Time

The Gift You Operate in a Lot of the Time and Modifies Your Primary Gift

Will Have Influence in Your Life but Not Like Primary & Secondary Gift

Indicates that You Have Not Adapted Well In Those Areas

The Three Part

Read Mark 12:30

In the same way the human being is made up of Spirit, Soul & Body, our soul is also triune in nature.
The three parts of the soul are the mind, the will and the emotions.
- The heart refers to the seat of emotions
- The mind refers to the thoughts
- The strength refers to the will

Read 1 John 2:16

The negative things that come from the three areas of the soul:
- Lust of the flesh – The emotions
- Lust of the eyes – The mind
- Pride of life – The will

The Three Part Nature

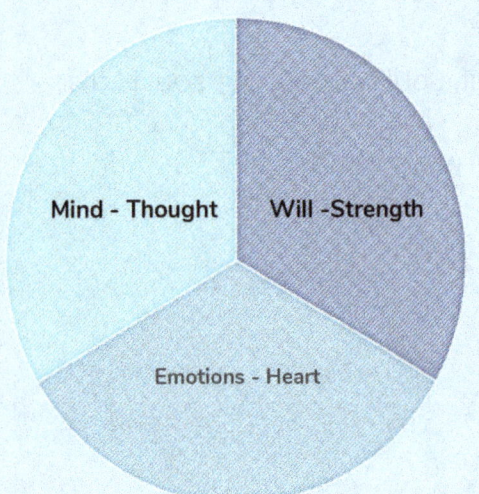

Note that three of the gifts operate out of and correspond directly to the mind, the will or the emotions

1. The Teacher gift operates primarily out of the mind area of the soul.
2. The Perceiver gift operates primarily out of the will area of the soul.
3. The Compassion gift operates primarily out of the emotions area of the soul.

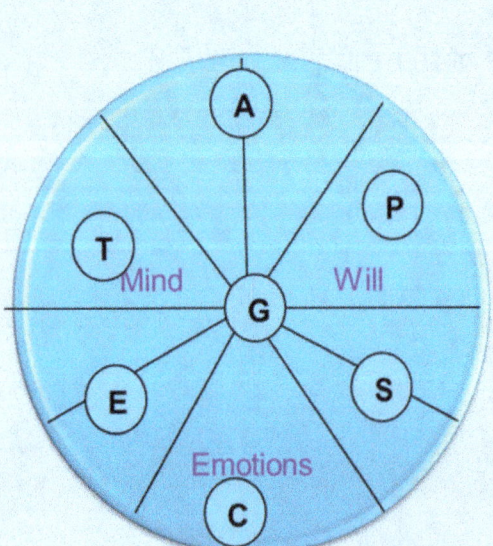

How Our Gifts Work Together

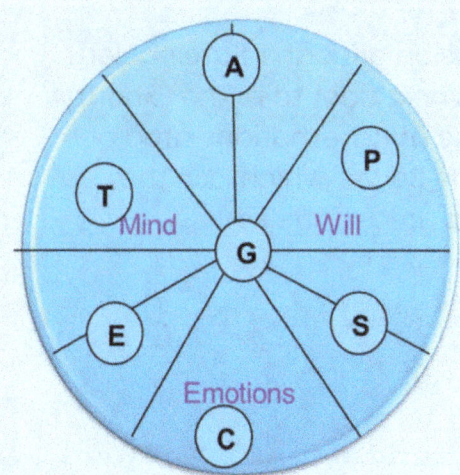

1. Three more of the gifts are influenced by and operate out of the two of the three areas of the soul.
2. The Administrator gift operates out of the mind and the will areas of the soul
3. The Exhorter gift operates out of the mind.
4. The Server gift operates out of the mind and emotions area of the soul
5. The seventh gift the giver gift operates about equally in all three areas

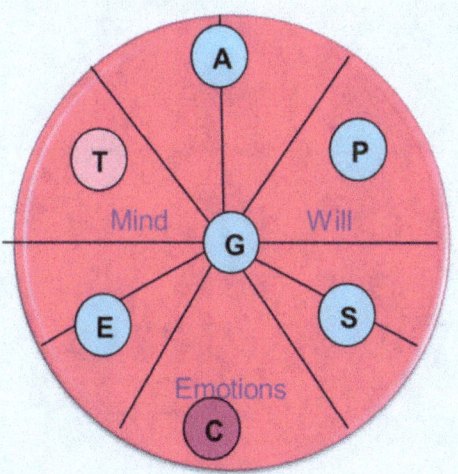

A Compassion gift will find it hard to cope with an Administrator gift (and vice versa).
An Administrator operates form the mind and will of the soul whilst the compassion gift operates from the emotions.
The gifts that fall into the triangular areas (Compassion, Teacher and Perceiver) also have some relationship challenges since they are still significantly different.

For example, the Compassion gift that operates from the emotions finds it hard to relate with the teacher gift that operates from the mind and the perceiver gift that operates from the will.

How Our Gifts Work Together

The Compassion gift can relate easier with the gifts next door to it. The Exhorter which is in the mind/emotions area of the soul or the Server which is in the will/emotions area of the soul.

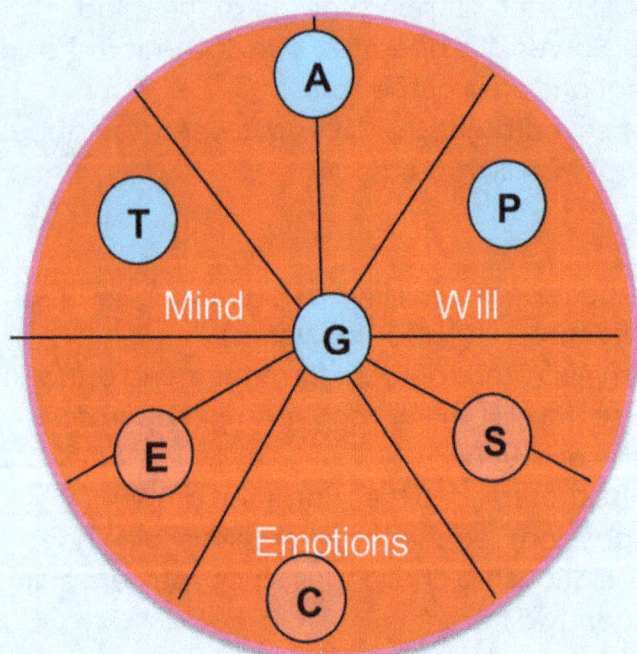

How Our Gifts Work Together

Draw in your own diagram and shade in the areas of the soul that influence your gifting, perspective and mode of operation.
Write your findings in your journal.

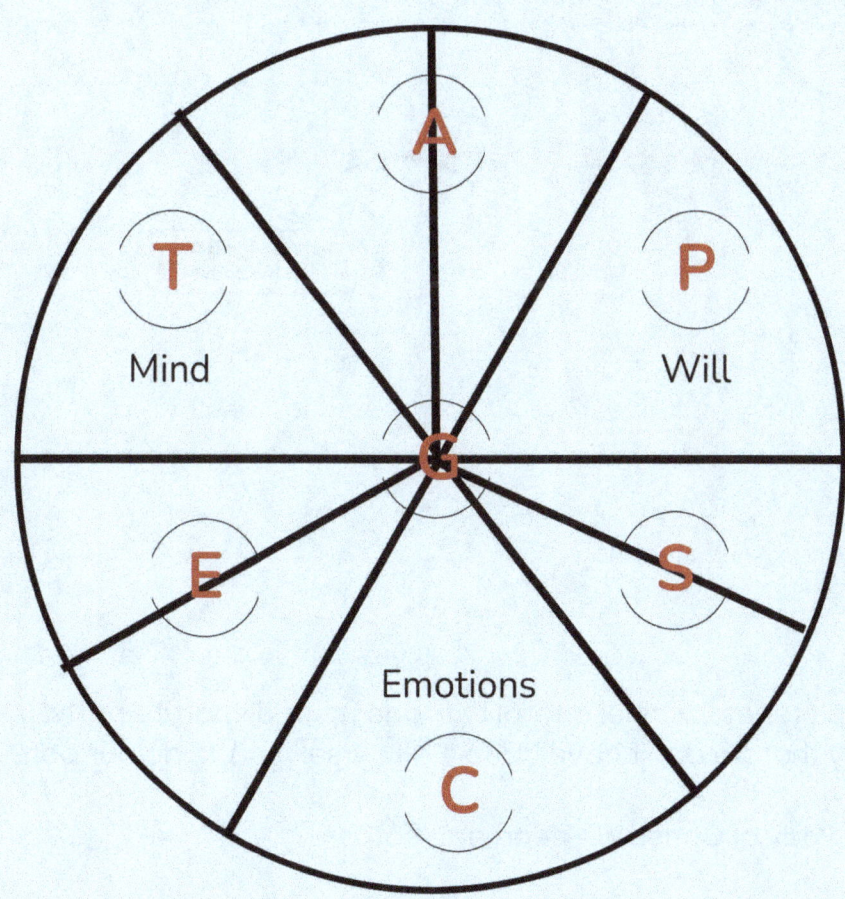

The Gifts In the Body

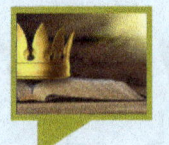

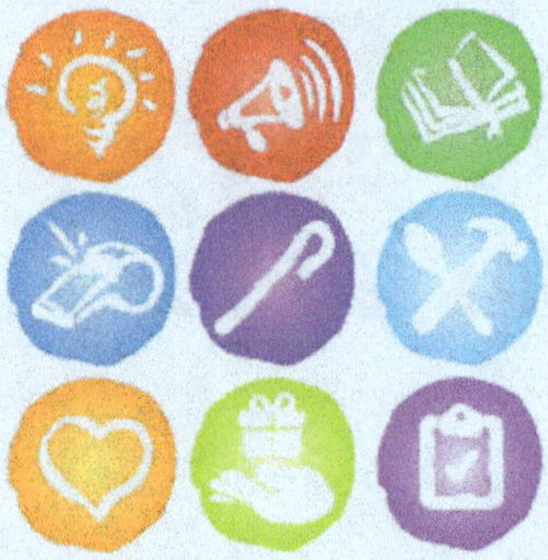

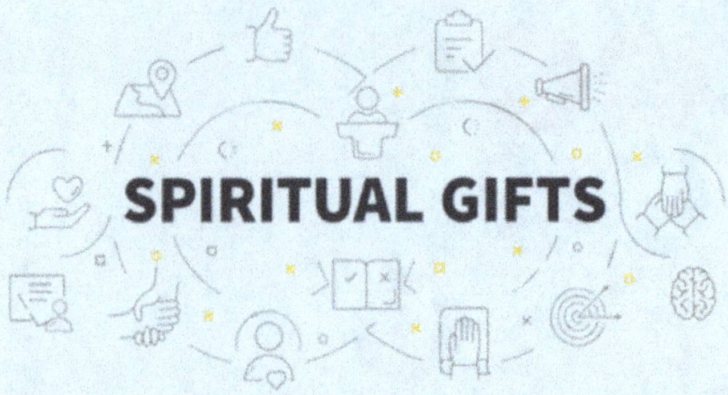
SPIRITUAL GIFTS

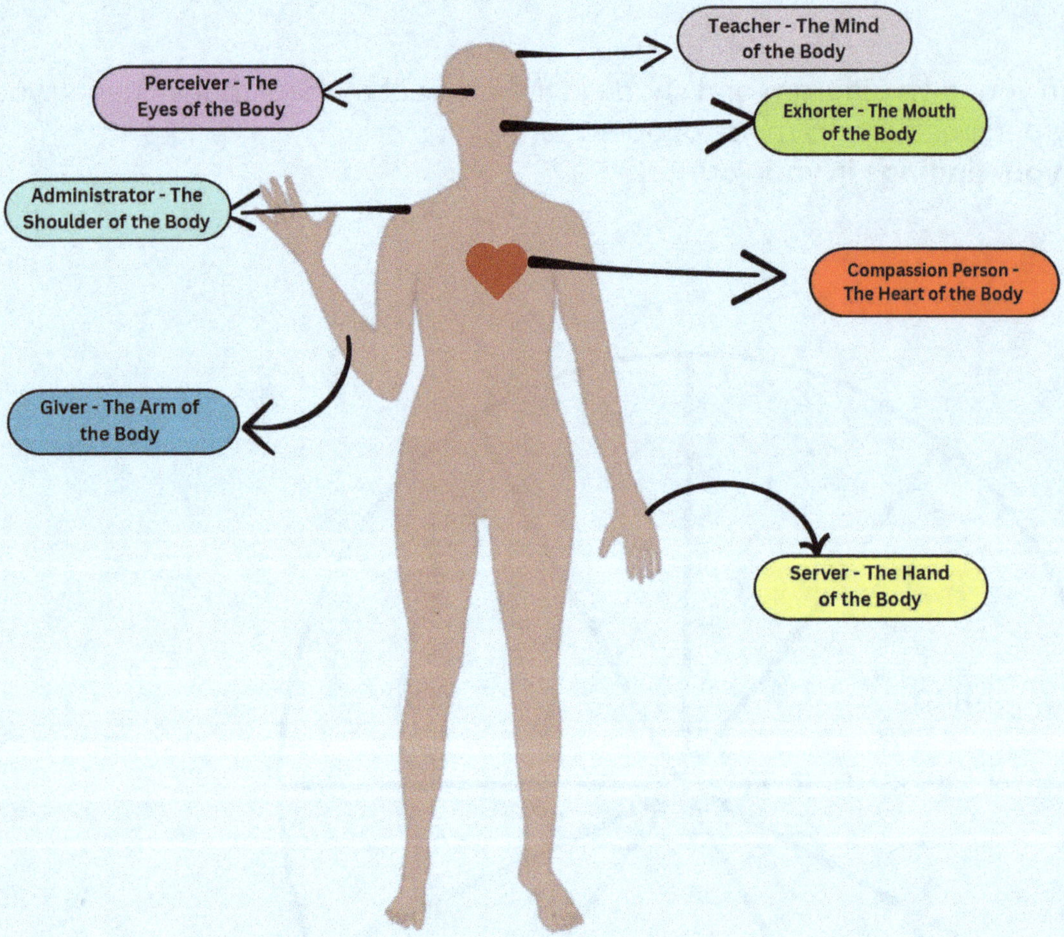
Teacher - The Mind of the Body
Perceiver - The Eyes of the Body
Exhorter - The Mouth of the Body
Administrator - The Shoulder of the Body
Compassion Person - The Heart of the Body
Giver - The Arm of the Body
Server - The Hand of the Body

The body represents completeness, whole; a totality made up of disparate parts. We can see in this analogy that we don't have to do it all ourselves. We do our part, others do their part.

We are dependent on the Body of Christ. We need each other.

- Have you completed Your Personal Gift Survey?
- What have you discovered to be your own gifts from the survey?
- What do the results mean for you and how to use them?
- What is your Manifestation Gifts?
- What is your Ministry Gifts?
- What is your Motivational Gifts?
- From a deep reflection (to include prayer) where do you believe God has positioned you in the Body and how you are to use these gifts in and for the Body?

Please use your reflection journal to continue

MODULE 5

Stirring Up Your Gift for Purpose

Kingdom Principles

For this reason I remind you to fan into flame (or stir up) the gift of God, which is in you through the laying on of my hands, for God gave us a spirit not of fear but of power and love and self-control.
2 Timothy 1:6

1. What did Paul mean by stirring up the gift?
2. What was this gift for?
3. Why did Timothy need to be encouraged?
4. What would you need to do if you were in Timothy's situation.

What's In Your Hand?

Moses and the Rod Exodus 4:2-17 Read.

Everyone has an ability to do something or to help someone.

An ability is the possession of the means or skill to do something and a talent, skill, or proficiency in a particular area.

What is a Skill? ...Something learned over time...	Effective Communicator
What is a Talent? Natural Ability	The ability to sing without training
What is a Gift? An intangible asset	Given by the Holy Spirit

Make a list of the abilities you believe you have to perform the different tasks you do daily? It could be in your job/career, at home as a mother, as a wife/husband, sister/brother, aunt/uncle, cousin, daughter/son.

All these abilities are used to build and to help others, whether you know what they are or not, you are useful and your abilities are necessary for others.
Ministry is all about using your abilities to help others.

Creating Capacity by Maximising Your Potential

God equips us to do something great with the SEED inside of us. This SEED is the abilities you possess (skills, talents, gifts).

Your potential is the ability to do great with what God has put inside you.

Maximising your potential means identifying the Seed in your possession and using it to the fullness of your ability. You are called to Steward the Seed and Multiply, this brings God glory.

The Parable of the Talents: Matthew 25:14-30 READ!

How would you advise someone with the challenge of wanting to do more for God, or their community?

Identifying Your Calling

Your Calling is God's invitation to participate in a specific way to bring Him glory. For example, if someone is gifted at graphic design, their calling is to use that gift in some way.

When you took the survey to discover your motivational gifts, you have essentially identified your calling. Your Calling is what you have in your hand and how you use what you have in your hand for your assignment and your purpose.

What is your God-given purpose, calling, and assignment? Throughout this session, we will dive deeper into: our Purpose (the WHY behind your new life), our Calling (the HOW we do it as you live out your new lives), and our Assignment (the WHAT you do as you surrender your lives to the leading of the Holy Spirit).

Purpose - The WHY behind your life
The reason for existence, or the "why" behind life. The first step is to discover PURPOSE. Rather than think about what you are here for, **think who am I here for**. Purpose is the overarching group or affected people you were put on earth to impact.

Calling - the HOW we do it as you live out your new lives
Once you sense the purpose, it's time to identify your CALLING. Your calling is a culmination of your skills, talents and gifts and is used to fulfil your purpose. **What unique skills, gifts, talents, resources, and/or personality** have you been given to use to impact your purpose. This would have been produced from both Gift Surveys in Module 4.

What's In Your Hand?

Assignment - the WHAT you do as you surrender your lives to the leading of the Holy Spirit
Now that you've determined who and how, the final step is to decide where or your ASSIGNMENT. **This is the role and place where the people of your purpose are and the practical role in which you will apply your calling.**

We experience a life of satisfaction and fulfilment when we are operating in our purpose, calling, and assignment. When we slip out of those areas, we feel the stress, burn out, discouragement, and unhappiness creep back in.

As a guide and example, I have included my PCA below. Note I did not discover this until I was 30 and I've clarified the calling and had many assignments in the last 10 years. I think it can be discovered much earlier, but that is my story.

My P, C, A
Purpose (Who): Empower Women to Fulfil their Purpose In Christ.
Calling (How): Prophetic Midwife, Mentor, Coach, Teacher, Perceiver, Exhorter, Wisdom, Knowledge, Faith.
Assignment (Where): Educational Institutions, Women in Business, Ministry and Marketplace

What Are You Here For? Examples of People Who Used What they Had...
- Feeding of the Five Thousand – John 6: 5- 12
- Moses and the Rod – Exodus 4: 2 – 5
- Joseph's dreams – Genesis 40-41
- The Woman with the Alabaster Box - Matthew 26:7
- The Widow with the Jar of Oil - 2 Kings 4:1-7

- Purpose - Who do I strongly sense I should be impacting with my life What group/circumstances of people am I deeply drawn to?
- Calling - In what unique way and/or with what unique talents, gifts, resources and/or skills can I use to impact the people that give my life purpose?
- Assignment - In what role and place can I use my unique way/talent/skills/gifts/resources to impact the people that give my life purpose?

(Please note, you probably will and can have multiple assignments over your life)
Please use your reflection journal to continue

_____
_____
_____
_____
_____
_____
_____
_____
_____
_____
_____
_____
_____
_____
_____
_____
_____
_____

What Is Ministry

Matthew 28:18-20 - **Read**
Corinthians 4:1-6 - **Read**
2 Timothy 2:15 - **Read**

Ministry is the faithful service of God's people rendered unto God and others on His behalf to bring Him glory, build up His church and reach out to His world.

In the New Testament, ministry is seen as service to God and to other people in His name. Jesus provided the pattern for Christian ministry - He came, not to receive service, but to give it.

Real ministry shines a light on what you already have in you.

Every seed bearing plant, has the ability to produce after its kind.

When you've discovered your own seed, when it's released, out of it will flow rivers of living water. **John 7:38 Read!**

Christians are to minister to others out of their devotion to Christ and their love for others, whether the other people are believers or unbelievers. Ministry to others should be impartial and unconditional, always seeking to help others as Jesus would. The ministry in our day has taken on more of a vocational meaning as we call pastors "ministers" to full-time service. Pastors do spend their lives in the ministry, they do minister to others, and they can rightly be designated as ministers, but pastors are not the only ones who are to be involved in ministry

Establishing the Principles of Seed Time and Harvest Time

God will use what you have, to transition you.
Identify the seed, then you will see the fruit.
Associate the seed with the fruit, then you will get a harvest.

Life began by the SEED Principle. In following God's principle of seed time and harvest, you must sow the seed of His Promise in the soil of your need.

Giving God your best entails sowing the **The Heart of Seed**
Unless you experience some sacrifice, you have not truly given.

How are you using your ability (seed) to the fullness of its potential for God?

1. Discover that potential (seed) He's put in you.
2. Use it to bless others.
3. As you develop in the fruits of the Holy Spirit, you are also able to reflect the righteousness of God in the lives of your others (clients, customers) etc.

What Is Ministry?

Ministry is not a mission trip, although that can be ministry. Ministry is not preaching from a pulpit, but it certainly can be. Ministry is not teaching a Sunday school class, but it can be. What is ministry then? It is as I stated before...letting God use you for the spreading of His word and will.

Cooking in a kitchen for homeless people can be a ministry, if you do it for the Glory of God. Scrubbing floors at a needy person's house can be a ministry...if you do it for the Glory of God. Are you catching on? People go on mission trips...but if their heart is not in the right place it is just action. People preach from pulpits, but if their heart is not right it is just words. People can teach Sunday school, but if their heart is not in it for God, then it is just a lesson. As the Bible says, do all things for the Glory of God that is ministry. If you approach it with that attitude, you will reflect the love of God.

It's only when you discover your gifts that you will have an indication of your purpose be it business, projects, entrepreneurial etc; as your ministry must reflect through that avenue.

An example of a character that used his ministry to identify and manage his gift to become an influential Prime Minister was Joseph. Explain!

How Skills, Talents & Gifts Work Together to Fulfil Your Purpose In Ministry

Your purpose is the desire birthed in your heart, you may not understand it because it's a dream as opposed to practical, the World tells us to stop dreaming and be real. That is a wrong statement to make.

God always works through our desires, those desires are actually His desires for us. Most times desires often come across as if they are out of reach, and such, may be unfamiliar in how we are to achieve what's in our hearts

Psalms 37:4

On the other hand, your calling is a combination of the abilities that you possess that you may not know of.
Your calling is practically what you have in your hand - your skills, talents and gifts. For example, your skills can be defined as those things that you have learnt overtime, quite possibly in a job, voluntary work or even at home etc; your talents are those things that you were born to do.

I normally refer to them as natural talents such as a talent for drawing or acting or even baking, these can also be described as gifts. Your purpose is what is in your heart your desires, dreams, aspirations. Your purpose is not really about you; it is bigger than you, it's about God fulfilling His purpose in and through you. When we make it all about us and not about Him, that's when things start falling apart. Marriage, family, life, work, finance and resources etc are all about purpose and not about us, He puts eternity in people's hearts therefore our talents and skills is about fulfilling God's purpose on earth.

How Skills, Talents & Gifts Work Together to Fulfil Your Purpose In Ministry.

Your calling is used to fulfil your purpose; you may find that difficult to comprehend, because fulfilling a purpose seems so distant, it's actually difficult to fulfil a dream you can perceive in your heart, but practically distant from you.

Your calling is the action plan used to fulfil that distant dream and bring it into a reality. That is why your daily activities be it work, voluntary, paid or unpaid, studying, work experience is used to develop your skills, gifts and talents.

A great example of a character whose gift was used to fulfil his purpose was Moses. He had a purpose in his heart to see his people free from slavery.

He wasn't an eloquent man, slow to speech, however when God asked him what he had in his hand, he saw it as an ordinary stick; but God took something ordinary and made it extra-ordinary; it became the Rod of God used to part the Red Sea where the Egyptians died and the Israelites where free to go.

Most times our skills, talents and gifts are not noticed easily because we devalue who we are.

Purpose (Heart) Vs Calling (Hand)

- What we have in our hand is a calling in the way of gifts, talents, skills. What we have in our hearts is something we would love to do.
- What we have in our hands involves pressure and discipline. What we have in our hearts is a dream, a sense of romance.
- What we have in our hands is now and familiar. What we have in our hearts is distant and mysterious.
- What we have in our hands can seem self indulgent i.e. my talent, my skills. What we have in our hearts is noble and all about making a difference.
- What we have in our hands looks like you and sometimes we may not like or accept how we look. What we have in our heart looks like the way we would like to look, i.e. famous actor, singer, entertainer or successful entrepreneur.

This is why people can sometimes devalue themselves; we see what we do as odds with what is in our hearts.

The main key is to be patient and faithful with what is in your hand and build on it and it will lead you to your purpose.

- What desires in your heart help you realise your purpose?
- What skills/gifts/resources in your hand help you to realise your calling?
- Describe your assignment?
- If you're having difficulty describing your assignment, think about the role and place of the people you speak to and perhaps deal with issues, and the practical things you do with your calling.
- Think about ways you can package your gift from the Gift Survey results
- Remember, this may be your children, parents, family members, work colleagues, clients.

Please use your reflection journal to continue

MODULE 6

Understanding and Overcoming Barriers to Spiritual Growth

Kingdom Principles

And a woman was there who had been subject to bleeding for twelve years, but no one could heal her. She came up behind him and touched the edge of his cloak, and immediately her bleeding stopped.
"Who touched me?" Jesus asked.
When they all denied it, Peter said, "Master, the people are crowding and pressing against you."
But Jesus said, "Someone touched me; I know that power has gone out from me."
Then the woman, seeing that she could not go unnoticed, came trembling and fell at his feet. In the presence of all the people, she told why she had touched him and how she had been instantly healed. Then he said to her, "Daughter, your faith has healed you. Go in peace." **Luke 8:43-48**

1. What does the story of the Woman with the Issue of Blood teach you about your own issues?
2. What is your understanding of faith in relation to this woman's actions?
3. What do you think God is doing in you to stretch your own faith to overcome your own issues?

What Is An Issue?

Everyone of us has been faced with some kind of issues, there are a few definitions of an issue, but for the sake of this programme, an issue sis defined as having problem that makes one unhappy and difficult to deal with.

There are many examples of issues in the Bible are main one is the Woman with the Issue of Blood, however Jesus was confronted with people with issues such as:

- The Samaritan Woman **John 4:7-25**
- The Man at the Pool of Bethsaida **John 5:1-9**
- The Woman about to be Stoned **John 8:3-11**

Jesus had compassion on those with issues, they didn't know how to overcome their issues, so they lived with it and in living with it made excuses.

When issues are not dealt with immediately, it creates a foundation for more layers of issues built up and eventually it creates a barrier that can prove a bigger problem in the heart.

God deals with us through our heart, He sees our heart and if there are barriers in our heart, it creates a barrier between us and God.

What Are Barriers?

Anything that holds apart, separates, or hinders progress or something that restricts, impedes, or blocks progress or the achievement of an ultimate objective or end.

It's necessary to know that barriers exist, we can experience issues in our life that can pose as a barrier.

When you discover your motivational gifts and want to stir it up by practising and using them, barriers can pose as a threat to using your gift, that is why it is important to identify the barriers to avoid delays in progression.

Examples of barriers

- Physical barriers

These are fixed or removable barriers that prevent entry, such as fences, traffic barriers, and crush barriers.

- Language barriers

These are barriers that occur when people have different levels of proficiency in a language, or when someone uses jargon that the other person doesn't understand.

- Emotional barriers

These are negative feelings about people, places, or situations that can prevent effective communication.

- Cultural barriers

These are barriers that arise from differences in language, beliefs, values, and behaviors.

- Perceptual barriers

These barriers can be overcome through personal efforts or changes in the cultural climate of a community.

- Technological barriers

These barriers occur when people don't have access to the necessary software, hardware, or other digital tools, or don't know how to use them

What Are Spiritual Barriers?

In Module 3 we discussed deliverance and you went through deliverance. As you know there are some issues that leave immediately once deliverance has been conducted, but there are some issues and barriers that leave overtime. We know by faith we are set free, but we also need to change our lifestyle to loving and living the word so that:

- Our mind is renewed daily by understanding God's will
- We can seek truth
- Removing whatever is blinding a person and preventing them from trusting God
- Convicting a person of sin, righteousness and judgement, and their need for a Saviour

You want to deal with anything that will present an obstacle in growing into a healthy Christian.

It's also important to understand that some barriers you will overcome as you pursue purpose.

What Are Spiritual Barriers?

We have dealt with deliverance and healing in Module 3. In this module we learn how to walk in our authority to kick some barriers out of the way so that we can move forward in our purpose, whether that is to start a ministry, write a book, set up a business for the Kingdom, prepare a group to attend to your nation, whatever it may be,

God wants you to build in peace and not in pieces, and as such you must understand your authority in Christ and mantle of responsibility.

The biggest obstacle in life are the barriers our mind creates, and most times the barriers we create in our mind comes from the fact that we don't believe that we can do what God is asking us to do. These barriers are referred to as spiritual barriers.

In essence a spiritual barrier is something that prevents a person from growing spiritually or being a healthy Citizen of the Kingdom. Some examples of spiritual barriers include:
Sins, Laziness, Bad company, False teaching, Weak preaching, An unhealthy church/ministry, and Ignorance. These barriers prevent growth and success as God desires because it affects our relationship with the Holy Spirit and how He is leading us to do the will of the Father.

God doesn't call the perfect, He calls the willing.

He also doesn't call you because you know it, He calls you because He wants to use your brokenness as a vessel to reach others and it is only through his Grace.

He also wants to keep you focused on His will, your ministry, while He works on your spouse and all that concerns your life for His purpose.

To confront or deal with barriers in your life is to seek exposure of the barrier and confront the root cause.

Sometimes it's not easy to confront the root cause if you're not prepared.

Overcoming Rejection

- **Turning to God**
Christians can turn to God in prayer and ask for his help in overcoming rejection. Prayer can help Christians feel accepted by Christ and build their inner strength.

- **Considering Jesus's example**
Jesus endured rejection and pain for the sake of others, and Christians can learn from his example. Acts 4:11 says that Jesus was "the stone which the builders rejected" but became "the cornerstone".

- **Seeing rejection as God's protection**
Some say that rejection and loss can help people understand who they are and who they are not.

- **Embracing faith**
Christians can have the courage to bring their faith forward in their lives and become ambassadors for Jesus.

He hears our cries and sees our needs. He doesn't leave us to flounder but enters our pain. Jesus endured pain and rejection for our sake. If the Saviour of the world can hold rejection in one hand and love for us in the other, then we can endure the pain rejection causes. The whole idea is to know that Jesus hasn't rejected you and you can overcome it knowing what He did for you and how much God loves you.

We will experience rejection, but Jesus is the "stone which the builders rejected" and he "has become the cornerstone" (Acts 4:11). With Jesus, the God of rejection and resurrection as our foundation, we too are resurrected after rejection. We have hope in Jesus Christ.

The bible is our mirror, the more we read it, the more we will see our true identity in Christ. Even Jesus said, "The one who listens to you listens to me. And whoever rejects you, rejects me. And whoever rejects me is rejecting God, who sent me" in Luke 10:16.

Pray about the experiences of rejection you have encountered and lean on the love of God

Overcoming Fear

- Pray: Ask God to reveal the root of your fear and to speak truth over it. You can also pray for help and declare that you trust God will help you.

- Read the Bible: Study, meditate on, and trust in the Word of God. You can memorize a verse to contradict the lies you've been believing.

- Replace fear with truth: Replace the lie of fear with the truth of God's Word.

- Partner with prayer warriors: Find people you trust to pray with you.

- Be patient: Retraining your mind to think differently about fear will take time.

- Remember who you are: Remember who you are and whose you are.

- Encourage yourself: Encourage yourself and refuse to speak curses over your life.

- Look beyond the surface: Look beyond the surface and discern the presence of God in every situation.

You can **pray out scriptures** as well whenever you are feeling fearful. Also, pray against that spirit or whatever limiting beliefs you are meditating on. Get to the **root** of what is causing you to fear. It is also good to pray that the Lord will give you the strength to overcome it. When you ask God to show you the root of where this fear comes from, it can happen immediately or in the mist of something you may be doing.

Prayers

Overcoming Shame

We live in this dangerous world and have the same instinct to hide ourselves.
Because sin is alive in our bodies (Romans 7:23) and because we are beset with weakness (Hebrews 5:2), the kind of shame we often experience is a potent combination of failure and pride.

We fail morally (sin), we fail due to our limitations (weakness), and we fail because the creation is subject to futility and doesn't work right (Romans 8:20). We also fail to live up to other people's expectations. And because we are full of sinful pride, we are ashamed of our failures and weaknesses, and will go to almost any length to hide them from others.
This means pride-fuelled shame can wield great power over us. It controls significant parts of our lives and consumes precious energy and time in avoiding exposure.

Like the woman at the well, King David, and the haemorrhaging woman, our shame frequently encourages us to hide in the wrong places.

We hide in our homes or away from our homes. We hide in our rooms and in our offices. We hide in housework, yard work, and garage puttering. We hide behind computers and phones and newspapers and magazines. We hide behind earphones and Netflix and ESPN. We hide behind fashion facades, education facades, career facades, Facebook facades, and pulpit facades. We hide in busyness and procrastination. We hide in outright lies or diversionary conversation. We hide behind sullenness and humour. We hide behind bravado and timidity. We hide in extroversion and introversion.

Just because pride moves us to hide our shame in the wrong places doesn't mean that our instinct to hide is completely wrong. It isn't. We do need a place to hide, but we need to hide in the right place.

Pray against the spirit of shame that you have encountered in your life at this point, so that you can move in purpose.

Overcoming Shame

There is only one place to hide that offers the protection we seek, where all our shame is covered and we no longer need to fear: the refuge of Jesus Christ (Hebrews 6:18–20). Jesus's death and resurrection is the only remedy for the shame we feel over our grievous sin-failures (Hebrews 9:26).

There is nowhere else to go with our sin; there is no other atonement (Acts 4:12). But if we hide in Jesus, he provides us a complete cleansing (1 John 1:9). And when that happens, all God's promises, which find their yes in Christ (2 Corinthians 1:20), become ours if we believe and receive them. And the grace that flows from these promises to us through faith are all-sufficient and abounding and provide for all our other shameful weaknesses and failures (2 Corinthians 9:8).

The key to breaking the power of pride-fuelled shame is the superior power of humility-fuelled faith in the work of Christ and the promises of Christ. Shame pronounces us guilty and deficient. Jesus pronounces us guiltless and promises that his grace will be sufficient for us in all our weaknesses (2 Corinthians 12:9–10). Christ is all (Colossians 3:11). As we trust Jesus as our righteousness (Philippians 3:9) and our provider of everything we need (Philippians 4:19), shame will lose its power over us.

That's what happened to the woman at the well. She listened to Jesus and believed in him, and her sin-wrecked life was redeemed and her shame destroyed.

That's what happened to King David. He confessed his sin and repented (2 Samuel 12:13) and trusted the pre-incarnate Christ, and his guilt and shame, which was great, was imputed to Christ and paid for in full.

That's what happened to the haemorrhaging woman. Jesus did make her tell the crowd about her shame, and in doing so she received the healing and cleansing she needed. Jesus made her shame a showcase of his grace.

Rejection, fear and shame if not uprooted can sabotage God's assignments in your life. Psalms 51

- How have you experienced rejection in your life
- How has fear revealed itself in your life?
- How has shame reflected in your life?
- How have you dealt with rejection, fear and shame so that it's not a barrier as you fulfil purpose?
- In order to move forward in fulfilling purpose what support must be in place for you to succeed?

Please use your reflection journal to continue

_____
_____
_____
_____
_____
_____
_____
_____
_____
_____
_____
_____
_____
_____
_____
_____

Understanding the Mantle of Responsibility

- *A 'mantle' is a Scriptural metaphor (symbol) for a calling, ministry, anointing and—when applicable—office, given to individuals by God.*
- *A mantle is not ours for the choosing, it is determined ahead of time by God. The desire God places in our hearts is just one indication, among other confirmations, of the calling that is ours.*
- *Ultimately, Joseph was robed in garments that represented his position as ruler next to Pharaoh in Egypt. (Gen 41:42) But he didn't go from being a youngster with prophetic dreams directly to the palace. He wore a succession of mantles, being faithful with each, and so it is for us.*

Although there are variations of the meaning of mantle in the Bible, the main idea is that of a covering such as a cloak or other article of clothing. The New American Standard Bible uses the word mantle in Joshua 7:21 and Hebrews 1:12. In the former passage, the ESV translates the word as "cloak" and, in the latter, "robe." In biblical times, a mantle was typically a large, loosely fitting garment made of animal skin, probably sheepskin. Several people are mentioned as wearing a mantle, including Job (Job 1:20) and Ezra (Ezra 9:5).

- Mantles are worn on the shoulders of the bearers as signs of carrying burdens and the weight of responsibilities.
- When a mantle is given to someone, it is a sign that the person has the ability and strength to shoulder responsibilities, tasks, assignments, heavy loads, and work.
- The mantle of Jesus Christ was governmental according to Isaiah the prophet: "For unto us a Child is born, unto us a Son is given; and the government will be upon His shoulder" (Isaiah 9:6).
- What your burden and area of calling is represents the mantle on your life. If you have a burden for healing, then essentially a "healing mantle" rests upon your life to see people healed. You will eat, sleep, and rest with a mantle of healing—it becomes part of your life's mission. The mantle and the bearer become one. You must become one with your mantle.

Understanding the Mantle of Responsibility

The word "mantle" is used in the Bible in several passages, including:
- Joshua 7:21: The ESV translates the word as "cloak"
- Hebrews 1:12: The ESV translates the word as "robe"
- 1 Samuel 15:27: Samuel is mentioned as wearing a mantle
- 2 Kings 2:14: Elisha takes the mantle that had "fallen" from Elijah

Before Elijah was translated into heaven, he said; "'Ask what I shall do for you before I am taken from you.' And Elisha said, 'Please, let a double portion of your spirit be upon me.'" (2 Kings 2:9) It was Elijah's mantle which proved whether or not Elisha received his request.

Elijah told him; "'You have asked a hard thing. Nevertheless, if you see me when I am taken from you, it shall be so for you; but if not, it shall not be so.'" (Verse 10) Elisha did see Elijah leave in a chariot of fire. He then tore his own garment in two pieces and "took up the mantle of Elijah that fell from him." (Verse 13) Thereafter, he also took up the work of his spiritual father and operated in his anointing.
Remember that Elisha asked for a double portion? And so it was.

The Bible records twice as many miracles for Elisha as are recorded under Elijah's ministry. Do spiritual mantles have a modern application? Can a spiritual mantle be passed today from one person to the next or one generation to the next?

Pray that you have a revelation of your mantle of responsibility and there will be no confusion

Understanding the Mantle of Responsibility for Greater Works

There is a wonderful precedent in the New Testament for those who desire to press in tight like Elisha did to Elijah. Jesus said; "'Truly, truly, I say to you, he who believes in Me, the works that I do shall he do also; and greater works than these shall he do; because I go to the Father.'" (John 14:12)

The anointing that is in Jesus is available to his followers and his mantle is greater than any prophet in the Old Testament. Seeking these "greater" works may manifest in an individual life in many ways depending on the gifts of the Holy Spirit deposited in them. One may have a healing anointing, another, a deliverance anointing, another, a gift of evangelism or gift of helps or administration. The mantle that you seek is usually the mantle that God wishes to impart.

What about a mantle passing from one person to another? Yes, I believe that happens. If God has placed someone in your life who is a giant in an area of Christian faith, you may seek to have their anointing and spiritual authority imparted to you. Maybe that is one of the reasons God has that person in your life. Remember though that the anointing resident in them is really a measure of God's Holy Spirit given to them by grace.

Spiritual mantles represent spiritual authority and they always have a cost. They also always demand great responsibility. A large mantle is not for the faint hearted or the immature.

Looking at your process and how God is stretching you, what Mantle do you believe He is preparing for you?

PAUSE & REFLECT

The Application of Right Standing

Matthew 6:31-34 READ!

Some say that right standing with God means:
- Having God's DNA
- Having the authority to pray and expect answers
- Having the authority to rebuke the devil and expect him to obey

Once you have accepted and received Jesus Christ as Lord and Saviour, you have been made righteous, which means you have Right Standing with God.

Right standing with God is the state of being in good standing with God at all times. It can be applied in several ways, including:

- **Forgiving sins**

Through faith in Jesus Christ, sinful people can have their sins forgiven and be placed in right standing with God.

- **Walking away from sin**

Once forgiven, people can choose righteousness and walk away from sin.

- **Living in righteousness**

People can live in the light of God's righteousness and bring glory to God.

- **Standing up for what's right**

People can use wisdom and discernment to stand up for what's right, and ask God for guidance.

- **Building confidence and trust**

Righteousness can build confidence and trust, and lead to enduring achievements.

The Application of Right Standing

The application of right standing means that every time of your life, you stand right with Him. You never stand wrong in the presence of God. It means you have God's DNA in you. It means you have authority to pray and expect answers.

 It means you have authority to rebuke the devil and expect him to obey. That is what right standing is. It means that you have been discharged and acquitted, the case is closed and it can never be appealed. There is nothing the devil can do about it. Why? Because you have a right standing

Your righteousness is not dependent on what you did right or wrong. It is a gift! A gift is not earned. You didn't earn it, you didn't deserve it and you didn't merit it. It was just given to you. All you do is to enjoy it. That is grace! Remember grace is unearned, unmerited and underserved. It is unconditional. It is not because you are being rewarded, No! It is predicated on God and God alone. It is God being good to you because He is good and gracious. It comes to you as a result of the death, burial and resurrection of Jesus.

Christ's righteousness is one of the things that grace has made available to us and it is time for the infallible proofs of those things in our lives to begin to manifest physically. It is not enough to have it in the spirit. No! It is time we begin to experience it in our lives and see it expressed in different areas of our lives. When you know what grace has brought into your life, you will no longer be a pushover for the devil. Knowing who you are in Christ also means knowing what Jesus purchased on your behalf and the benefits of His death burial and resurrection.

Romans 5:16-21 READ
Romans 10:4 READ

The Righteous Test

Please complete the Righteous Test to discover where you are in right standing

Righteous Act	Meaning	Yes	No	Room for Improvement
Hardworking	The righteous do not fear hard work, and their work is successful through the righteousness of God			
Forgiving	The righteous are forgiving, even as God forgave them			
Kind	The righteous are kind and tenderhearted.			
Faithful	The righteous are faithful in their worship			
Virtuous	The righteous live a virtuous life.			
Fair	The righteous play fair The			
Respectful	righteous respect authority.			
Reverent	The righteous revere God's will			
Courageous	The righteous have the courage to stand.			
Obedient	The righteous are completely obedient in glorifying God			
Orderly	The righteous order their lives according to God's laws			

- What has been the areas in your life that God has been processing in and through you?
- What do you believe is your mantle of responsibility?
- What would you be your approach to work on those areas of weakness?
- Looking at your process and how God is stretching you, what Mantle have you identified that He is preparing for you?
- Have you taken the righteous test, what improvements do you need to work on and through?
- How would you implement these improvements

Please use your reflection journal to continue

MODULE 7

Occupy Your Promise Land

Kingdom Principles

Then I saw "a new heaven and a new earth," for the first heaven and the first earth had passed away, and there was no longer any sea. I saw the Holy City, the new Jerusalem, coming down out of heaven from God, prepared as a bride beautifully dressed for her husband. And I heard a loud voice from the throne saying, "Look! God's dwelling place is now among the people, and he will dwell with them. They will be his people, and God himself will be with them and be their God. 'He will wipe every tear from their eyes. There will be no more death'[b] or mourning or crying or pain, for the old order of things has passed away."
Revelations 21:1-4

1. What does the new heaven and new earth represent?

2. Why is the new Jerusalem represented as a Bride?

3. Why would God wipe away the tears of His People?

4. What was the old order of things?

Occupy Your Promise Land

Luke 19: 11-13 Read!
Matthew 25:14-30 Read!

The only way we can occupy the inheritance (Land) that God has given us is by understanding who we are in Him which you studied in Module 2 and understanding what our gifts are and how to use them, that is why when we come into the Kingdom, the process to build is about developing and becoming mature in Christ, otherwise we mess up and make God look like a charlatan.

God is not a charlatan and can never be, but what we must understand is that we are developed, taught and trained to be a good steward of the inheritance He has for us.

The word "occupy" means to be busy or to invest with the intent of increasing something. Jesus is telling his followers to take care of business and not worry about the future kingdom.

The parable in Luke 19 is about a nobleman who leaves ten of his servants with money and instructs them to invest it wisely while he is away. When he returns, he finds that some of the servants have worked hard to increase his wealth and rewards them. The other servant hid the money away out of fear and the nobleman punishes him.

Group Discussion Activity

Luke 16: 1-14 Read
The master was going to remove the steward from his job, but he thought within himself and did something to turn his situation around.
How is this applicable in your present situation, about occupying?

The Change Agent

As a disciple you're called to emulate the principles of Christ and embrace His Teachings and model your life after His examples.

What Is a Change Agent?

A change agent is someone who impacts the status quo through their influence negatively or positively. A change agent **helps an organization or group embrace and carry out change**. They can also be called change champions, change influencers, or agents of change.

As God's change agent, you are called to introduce Kingdom change within the spheres of your assignment. actively promotes and facilitates transformation. They have vision, leadership, an action-oriented mindset, the ability to collaborate and inspire others, and empathy, actively promotes and facilitates transformation.

Examples:

- Charles Darwin
- Pluto
- Rosa Parks
- Adolph Hitler
- Saddam Hussein

Personal Reflection and Exercise

Provide an example of who you consider to be a Change Agent and explain why you think they're a Change Agent

142

Six Stages of The Change Agent Process

The Change Agent Process

1. Recruitment
2. Character Development
3. Isolation
4. The Cross
5. Problem Solving
6. Networks

1st Stage - Recruitment

- Where adversity and often betrayal, a waiting period and perseverance are part of the character development
- God helps us in a process of moving out of slavery, helps us from being orphans to being Sons and Daughters.
- That's why many would say though I am having a difficult season, but spiritually it's the greatest, because He is revealing Himself in ways like never before

1st Stage - Recruitment

- Recruitment through divine circumstances
- Moses' encounter at the Burning Bush
- King Saul – Samuel the Prophet
- Paul – blinded by Jesus on the road to Damascus
- Recruitment through conflict, which causes us to enter into the larger story.
- David & Goliath – he delivered food to delivering a nation
- Martin Luther King – wrestled with salvation
- Change Agents are not looking to be change agents, however God requires a person to obey and do His Will, that's why the recruitment can be a challenge for those who are standing for a loved one. Certainly not challenging for God.

Six Stages of The Change Agent Process

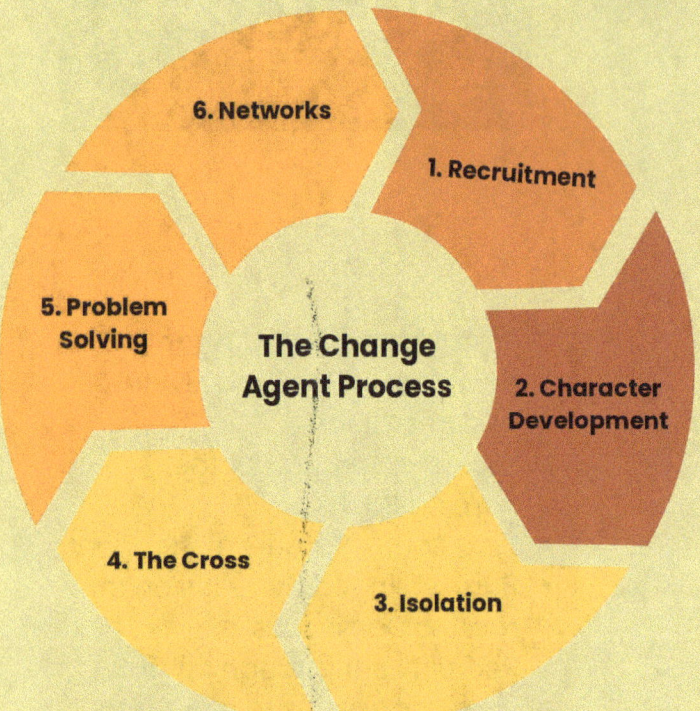

2nd Stage – Character Development
- If God leaves us for a short season in the wilderness we will only change the habit and go back to our old ways.
- Even going to the place of Promise, we will still have to fight spiritual warfare, this involves faith experiences and provision is directly related to obedience not sweat and toil.
- What does the Promise Land look like?
- Joseph Calling...
- He had a spiritual and physical calling on his life to be a provider through adversity. God sent him ahead of time to serve a nation.
- Joseph was a physical picture of Jesus, betrayed by his own people and who became a provider

2nd Stage – Character Development
- Joseph had four major tests
- Betrayal – every leader that will be used by God would experience betrayal, because Jesus had to wash the feet of Judas who betrayed Him. Betrayal is so difficult because we cannot forgive people who have betrayed us in our own flesh
- Sexual – Joseph passed the sexual test. He was a faithful man and the only way he was able to pass by fleeing.

Six Stages of The Change Agent Process

The Change Agent Process
1. Recruitment
2. Character Development
3. Isolation
4. The Cross
5. Problem Solving
6. Networks

2nd Stage – Character Development
- Romans 12:2 Read
- The journey to the Promise Land of a transformed mind requires many stepping stones.
- Psalm 127:1 Read
- We were born into slavery because of the sin nature, but God wants us to come out of Egypt (sweat and toil)
- Joshua 9:14
- Joshua had to repent and uphold the Covenant.
- God is very big on Covenant
- God will not change your circumstances until there is a nature change.

2nd Stage – Character Development
- Joseph had four major tests
- Perseverance – Joseph goes through the process for many years even though he interpreted the Cup Bearer's dream.
- Stewardship – would Joseph make amends by getting revenge to pay back the Cup Bearer and his brothers
- God is very strategic, He makes mess-ups as if it was all part of His plans.
- Personal crisis is always the first chapter of the larger story of our lives
- God helps us in a process of moving out of slavery, helps us from being orphans to being Sons and Daughters.
- That's why many would say though I am having a difficult season, but spiritually it's the greatest, because He is revealing Himself in ways like never before

Six Stages of The Change Agent Process

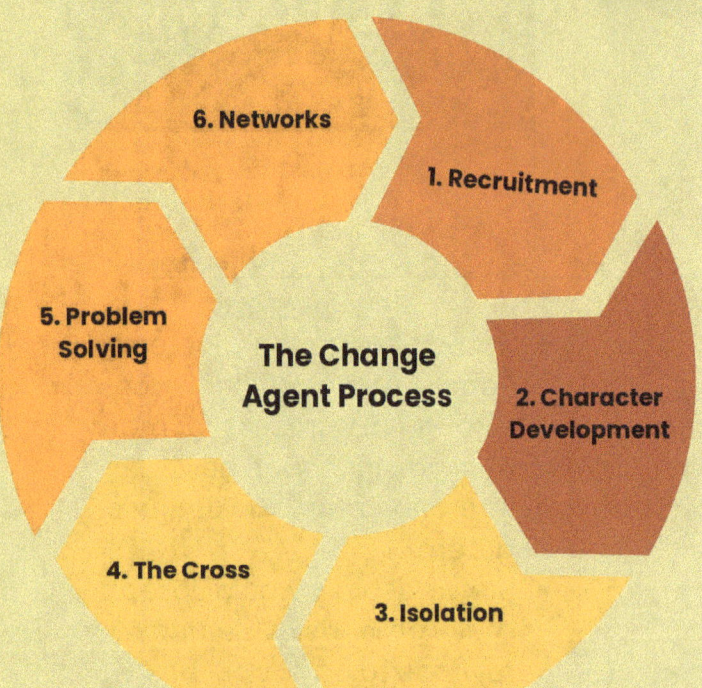

3rd Stage – Isolation Period
- God initiates a time of separation from past dependencies to realign values.
- 1st Samuel 22:1 Read
- David's training period was fleeing Saul's sword. When you do a job very well, there is a lot of jealousy.
- In Adullam, David is at the darkest place of his life because he had to fake madness.

- David would have had the kind of thoughts sitting in the cave, wondering how life got him to were he was.
- He thinks back to when Samuel anoints him to be king and it seems circumstances are not lining up with the prophetic word.
- What do you do when things don't line up to the word you received?
- David wrote three Psalms in the Cave.
- The Cave is often an example of messes being turned into messages.
- Isaiah 45:3
- Matthew 10:27-28
- Psalm 31:20
- Apostle John was banished to the Island of Patmos where he wrote the book of Revelations
- Paul was hidden away for 3 years in Arabia before he was released into his assignment
- Elijah was fleeing for his life from Jezebel, when the word of the Lord came to him

Six Stages of The Change Agent Process

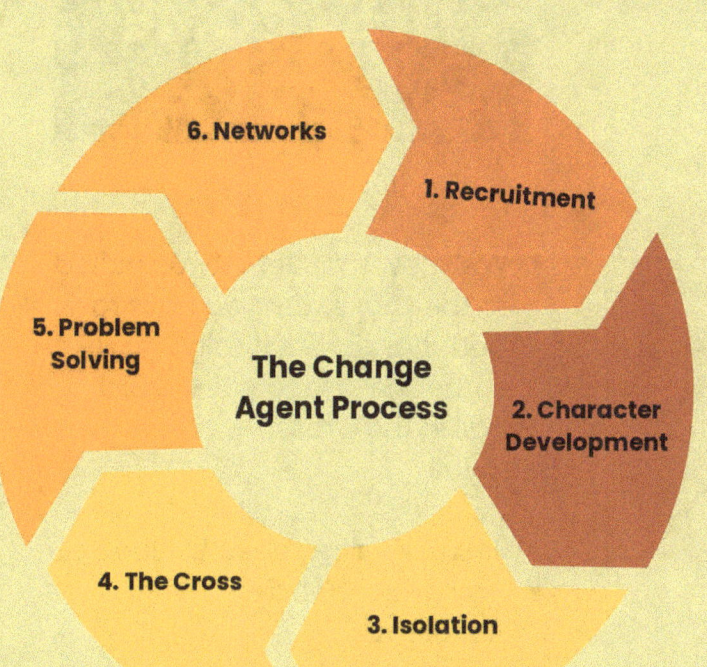

3rd Stage – Isolation Period
- Often, dark places brings revelation
- Job 12:22
- Jeremiah 33:3
- Daniel 2:22
- What God desires in that isolation period is to make deposits and a greater intimacy with Him.
- Psalm 31:14
- Can we trust Him in the times of waiting?

3rd Stage – Isolation Period
- God initiates a time of separation from past dependencies to realign values.
- 1st Samuel 22:1 Read
- David's training period was fleeing Saul's sword. When you do a job very well, there is a lot of jealousy.
- In Adullam, David is at the darkest place of his life because he had to fake madness.

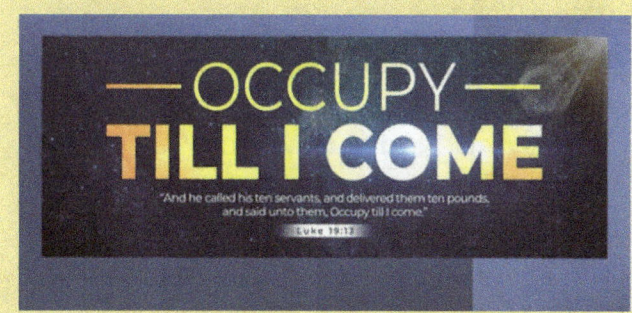

Six Stages of The Change Agent Process

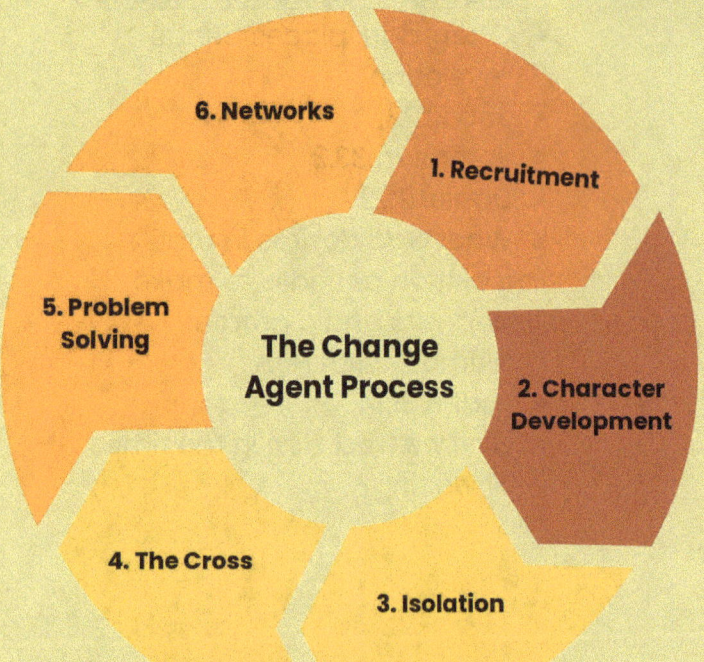

- We know that Jesus was nailed to the Cross with two nails to both hands, but it takes someone else to put the 3rd nail in the Cross.

Betrayal!

- Jesus was betrayed by Judas
- David was betrayed by Absalom
- Joseph was betrayed by his Brothers
- God has to disqualify you from thinking you are qualified for the mission He has for you.
- Sometimes a man finds his destiny on the road he most seeks to avoid.
- •Crisis and pain leads to greater commitment, obedience and intimacy
- Micah 4:6-7
- Pain is designed to encourage obedience that leads to intimacy with God.
- Psalm 119:67
- Hebrews 5:8-9

4th Stage - The Cross
- There has to be the place where the old has died or the new to live.
- God takes the change agent through a series of character tests designed to develop humility, trust and intimacy with God.
- Galatians 2:20 Read

Six Stages of The Change Agent Process

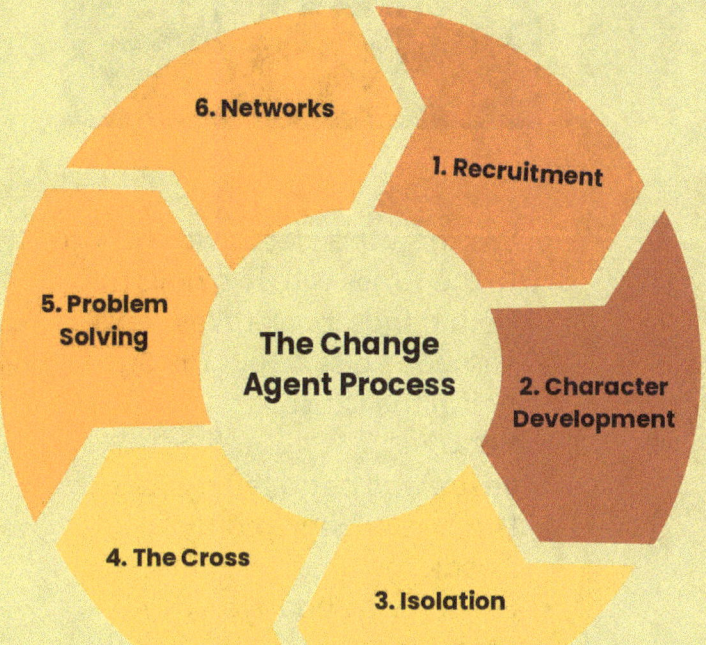

4th Stage - The Cross
- There has to be the place where the old has died or the new to live.
- God takes the change agent through a series of character tests designed to develop humility, trust and intimacy with God.
- Galatians 2:20 Read

4th Stage - The Cross
- We know that Jesus was nailed to the Cross with two nails to both hands, but it takes someone else to put the 3rd nail in the Cross.
- Betrayal!
- Jesus was betrayed by Judas
- David was betrayed by Absalom
- Joseph was betrayed by his Brothers
- God has to disqualify you from thinking you are qualified for the mission He has for you.
- Sometimes a man finds his destiny on the road he most seeks to avoid.
- Crisis and pain leads to greater commitment, obedience and intimacy
- Micah 4:6-7
- Pain is designed to encourage obedience that leads to intimacy with God.
- Psalm 119:67
- Hebrews 5:8-9

Six Stages of The Change Agent Process

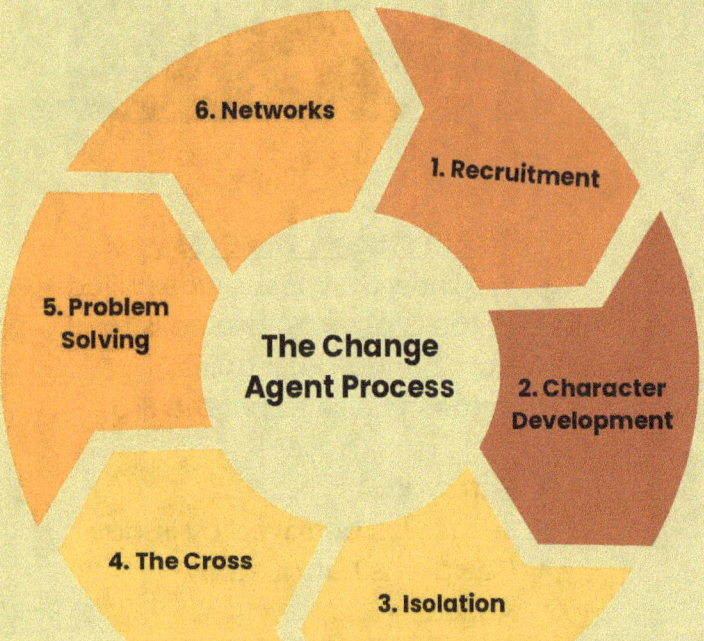

- We know that Jesus was nailed to the Cross with two nails to both hands, but it takes someone else to put the 3rd nail in the Cross.
- Betrayal!
- Jesus was betrayed by Judas
- David was betrayed by Absalom
- Joseph was betrayed by his Brothers
- God has to disqualify you from thinking you are qualified for the mission He has for you.
- Sometimes a man finds his destiny on the road he most seeks to avoid.
- Crisis and pain leads to greater commitment, obedience and intimacy
- Micah 4:6-7
- Pain is designed to encourage obedience that leads to intimacy with God.
- Psalm 119:67
- Hebrews 5:8-9
- The higher you go up in the mountain of influence, the greater the scrutiny.

4th Stage - Personal Cross

- There has to be the place where the old has died or the new to live.
- God takes the change agent through a series of character tests designed to develop humility, trust and intimacy with God.
- Galatians 2:20 Read

Six Stages of The Change Agent Process

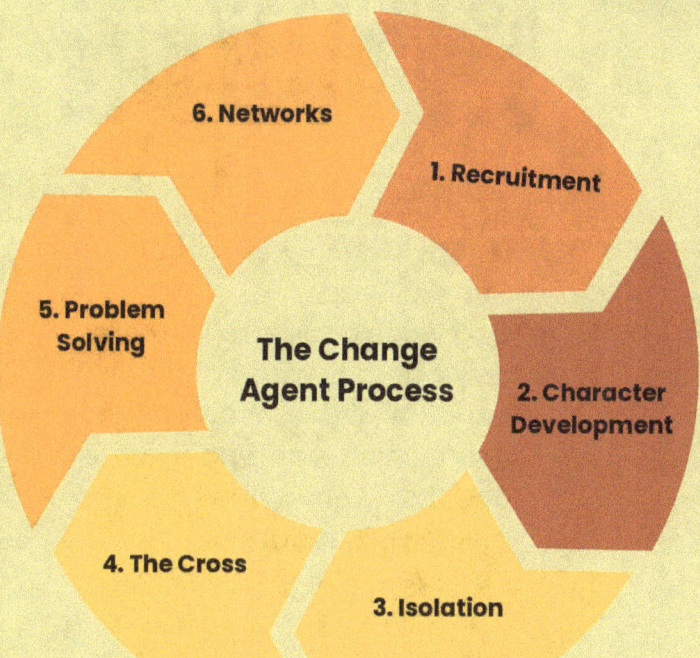

- David had a spiritual call which was the need to stand up to Goliath, but he also had another side to him.
- He had a small business and along with the business came the following perks.
- King's daughter
- No taxes
- Great Wealth
- Understood Covenant
- David had an understanding of Covenant.
- When he went up against Goliath, he was a representative of God to enforce the covenant
- At a very young age Joseph had incredible understanding
- Gen 41:38/39
- Why did Pharaoh say this to Joseph? Joseph had a solution
- When you come with a solution, you become the person of influence.
- Gen 41:38-41 Read
- God has something in you He wants to birth to solve a problem

5th Stage - Problem Solvers

- Change Agents are often problem solvers through invention and entrepreneurship.
- God has to have a people He can steward.

Six Stages of The Change Agent Process

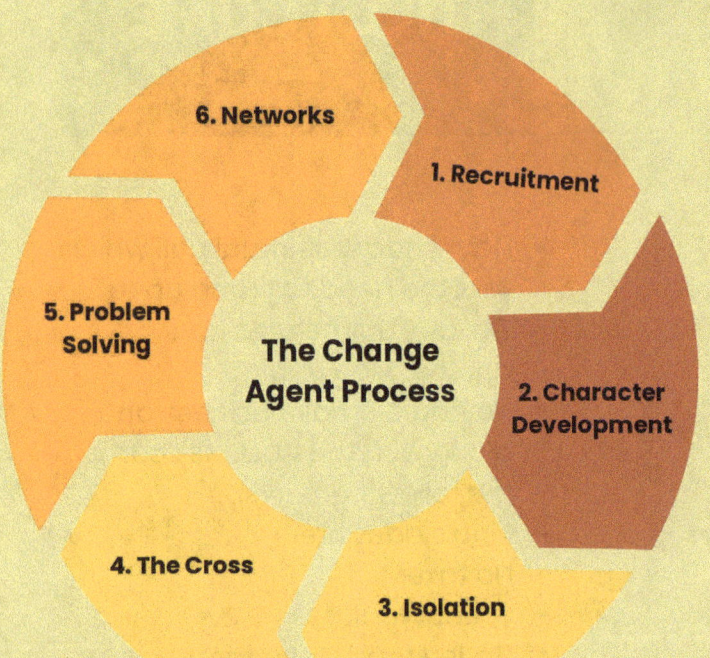

6th Stage - Networks

- Gen 11:6 Read
- God wasn't going to let them do what they wanted to do because of the motives of the heart which was a pride issue and they were trying to build their own kingdom.
- However what is noticeable was the power of moving as one. Nothing is impossible to you when you work as one.
- John 17:20-22 Jesus' prayer focused on being one
- When we leverage and stop building our own individual ideologies we would see a response to the gospel like never before and God starts moving in our midst.

6th Stage - Networks

- God believes in teams exemplified by the trinity

- What stage of the Change Agent design process do you recognise yourself to be at?
- What process helps you to identify that you're at the stage you have identified?
- What challenges are you facing at the stage you have identified?
- How is your walk with God helping you to overcome those challenges at the stage you have identified?

Please use your reflection journal to continue

_____
_____
_____
_____
_____
_____
_____
_____
_____
_____
_____
_____
_____
_____
_____
_____
_____

The 7 Mountains of Influence

Isaiah 2:2 Read

The bible tells us that there will be a sheep and a goat nations. Sheep represent those who follow Christ and goats represents those who follow other gods.

All the nations will be gathered before him, and he will separate the people one from another as a shepherd separates the sheep from the goats. (Matthew 25:32)

Arts & Entertainment
- Enemy: Hivites
- Principality: Jezebel
- Authority: Prophets
- Mission: Model greater creative arts of God and prophesy through them
- Key: Glory

Business
- Enemy: Canaanites
- Principality: Mammon
- Authority: Prophets
- Mission: Discover and transfer wealth into kingdom purposes
- Key: Riches

Education
- Enemy: Amorites
- Principality: Beelzebub
- Authority: Teachers
- Mission: Bring in new fear of God based curriculum
- Key: Wisdom

Religion
- Enemy: Perizzites
- Principality: Religious Spirit
- Authority: Holy Spirit
- Mission: Model Holy Spirit infused life and ministry
- Key: Honor

Media
- Enemy: Hittites
- Principality: Apollyon
- Authority: Evangelists
- Mission: Fill airwaves with "good news"
- Key: Blessing

Government
- Enemy: Girgashites
- Principality: Lucifer
- Authority: Apostles
- Mission: Fill government with humble, servant leaders
- Key: Power

Family
- Enemy: Jebusites
- Principality: Baal
- Authority: Pastors
- Mission: Impact social system so family unit is prioritized
- Key: Strength

7 mountains of influence

The 7 Mountains of Influence

Joshua and the 7 Enemies

Then Joshua commanded the officers of the people, saying, "Pass through the camp and command the people, saying, 'Prepare provisions for yourselves, for within three days you will cross over this Jordan, to go in to possess the land which the Lord your God is giving you to possess.'" (Joshua 1: 10-11)

7 Nations Greater and Mightier

"When the Lord your God brings you into the land which you go to possess, and has cast out many nations before you, the Hittites and the Girgashites and the Amorites and the Canaanites and the Perizzites and the Hivites and the Jebusites, **seven nations greater and mightier than thou"** (Deuteronomy 7:1).

Displace 7 Enemies (Mountains) to take the Promise Land

"This is how you will know that the living God is among you and that He will certainly drive out 7 enemies before you including the Canaanites, Hittites, Hivites, Perizzites, Girgashites, Amorites and the Jebusites" (Joshua 3:10).

Reclaiming Your Mountain of Influence

The earth is the Lord's, and everything in it, the world, and all who live in it (Psalm 24: 1).

God created man to take dominion over the fish of the sea, the birds of the air and over the cattle and over all the earth and over every creeping thing that creeps upon the earth (Genesis 1:26). That means as Change Agents, when you've been restored back to Jesus, you automatically have dominion over all that God has given you, you're called to Steward what has been given to you.

God's original intent was for all individuals and nations to be blessed through obedience (Deuteronomy 28:1-14)

- To prosper in every way
- To fulfil your unique purpose
- To fulfil God's overall plan
- To receive your God ordained inheritance
- For all creation to reflect His Glory

Furthermore to reclaim the Mountains of Influence you have to believe in you that you are the head and not the tail. The LORD will make you the head, not the tail. If you pay attention to the commands of the LORD your God that He has given you this day and carefully follow them, you will always be at the top, never at the bottom. (Deuteronomy 28:13-14) (Let's pause and reflect on this promise)

This is achieved through servant leadership, not legislation or political activism

Reclaiming Your Mountain of Influence

How was Dominion Lost in the Garden?

We know that God gave man dominion on the birds of the air, the fish in the sea and every creepy animal that is on earth. God had relationship with Adam and walked with him in the cool of the day.

However, Satan deceived Eve, who also deceived Adam and this dominion that was given to them was given to Satan.

Disobedience was how they lost their dominion.

God's Redemption Plan

Jesus came to claim to reclaim what Satan took in the Garden. God has a redemption plan that was lost through our own disobedience, ignorance, immaturity, foolishness etc. And as Jesus reclaim all that was lost, we also enforce our claim through Christ.

"For the Son of Man has come to seek and to save *that* which was lost"(Luke19:10).

"For God was pleased to have all His fullness dwelling in Him, and through Him to reconcile to Himself *all things*, whether things on earth or things in heaven, by making peace through His blood, shed on the Cross" (Colossians 1:19-20).

This also includes your Marriage, and there is a strategy through Christ to Stand for a Restored Marriage and it is through your Salvation. He Calls You In Righteousness...

The Original Intent Through Moses

Not to establish a religion but a nation of people who would love, serve, and honour God.

But you are a chosen generation, a royal priesthood, a holy nation, His own special people, that you may proclaim the praises of Him who called you out of darkness into His marvellous light (1Peter 2:9-10)

Most times we operate in religion and not Kingdom and religion opens the door to the enemy, Jezebel, Leviathan, Pride, Witchcraft, Control and many other negative influences. To deal with these issues in you, **please revisit Module 3 of this Workbook.**

How We Lost the Mountains (Including the Family Mountain which is where Marriage resides)

1. Separation from God - Solution Humble Ourselves and Pray **(2 Chronicles 7:14)**
2. The Gospel of Salvation Vs The Gospel of the Kingdom - Solution Stopping at Salvation is like Sitting Down After Crossing the Jordan! There is a need to Occupy and Not Be Left Behind **(Luke 19:13)**
3. Unbiblical View of Work and Ministry - Solution What Does the Word Say about Work. What Are You Called to Do In Your Job (Mountain)? **(Colossians 3:23-24)**

How God Prepares Leaders to Reclaim Mountains

1. **Calling Before Clarity**
You're process prepares and chooses you out for leadership.

God often calls us before we feel qualified or ready. Like Moses at the Burning Bush or David anointed while still a shepherd. He sees our destiny before we do.

Your process **"chooses"** you because God has already **chosen you**, and the process begins to unfold in alignment with that call.

2. **The Wilderness Season: Preparation Through Pressure**
Before stepping into leadership, many go through a wilderness or hidden season - a time of testing, isolation and growth. Think of the following people in the bible:
- **Joseph** in prison before the palace
- **David** in caves before the crown
- **Jesus** in the wilderness before public ministry

> And after you have suffered a little while, the God of all grace will himself, restore, confirm, strengthen, and establish you
> 1 Peter 5:10

> You did not choose Me, but I chose you and appointed you that you should go and bear fruit -
> John 15:16

These seasons strip away self reliance and build humility, trust and obedience. It's in the wilderness that your character catches up with your calling.

3. **Pain Becomes Purpose**
The hardships, betrayals, delays and lessons you walk through aren't random. They become the very tools God uses us to develop compassion, wisdom and discernment in you. Your pain positions you for leadership because it gives you authority to speak into others' lives with authenticity

How God Prepares Leaders to Reclaim Mountains

4. **Faithfulness in the Small Things**
God watches how you handle small assignments, obscure roles, and hidden acts of obedience. Your willingness to serve, even when unseen or uncelebrated, reveals your heart.

This is often when the process chooses you - because you've proven trustworthy, not through ambition, but through surrender.

5. **Anointing Follows Brokenness**
Kingdom leadership doesn't come from striving, titles, or platforms. It flows from a life of surrendered to God, often broken but yielded, like the alabaster jar poured out in worship. Your process becomes the proving ground, the refining fire and ultimately the qualification because it shows you've let God form Christ in you.

The process chooses you because God uses it to align your inner life with His purposes. It's not about your ability but your availability, not your gifting but your heart. If you are in a hard or hidden season now, know this

You're not being overlooked, you're being prepared

> ***Whoever can be trusted with very little can also be trusted with much Luke 16:10***

Joseph – A Model for Occupying the Government Mountain

How Joseph became Prime Minister of Egypt was only by the Hand of God. He knew his gift and his skill and though his family didn't take it seriously, it was the very thing that God used to propel him into his destiny for God's Purpose.

Scripture Reference - Genesis 37; 39 – 46

Let's study the model Joseph used in occupying the Government Mountain.

1. He understood, mastered and used his gift - Dreams.
2. Adversity - 13 years of character development, moral purity, perseverance and forgiveness.
3. Operated in the Supernatural - dreams, words of knowledge, words of wisdom
4. Planted him near a key influencer - Pharaoh
5. Leadership Skills - he allowed God work through and in him as the leader
6. Awaited the timing of God for advancement - he was able to steward resources

Deborah - A Model for Occupying the Family Mountain

Deborah is a powerful biblical model for occupying the family mountain. Her life demonstrates how God can raise someone to heal, govern and nurture not just a nation, but also its spiritual and familial order.

Scripture Reference - Judges 4-5

Let's study the model Deborah used in occupying the Family Mountain

1. She understood and mastered her position, role, gift and skill - Prophetess/Judge
2. Prophetess - she heard from God and gave direction
3. Judge - a civic leader and decision maker for Israel
4. Mother of Israel. Not just metaphorically - this title reflected her role nurturing a broken nation back to order (Judges 5:7)
5. Wife of Lappidoth - she functioned in public leadership without compromising her home identity.
6. This reveals the power of spiritual motherhood - to awaken courage, nurture identity, and
7. call people into destiny. On the Family Mountain, this represents:
8. Restoring broken family identity
9. Nurturing faith and obedience
10. Covering people with prayer and direction like a spiritual midwife

Your Land Shall Be Married

This session equips women standing for marriage restoration to walk in renewed hope, identity, and prophetic alignment with God's covenant promises.

Our scripture reference is taken from Isaiah 62:4

Isaiah 62:4 (NKJV) – "You shall no longer be termed Forsaken, nor shall your land any more be termed Desolate; but you shall be called Hephzibah, and your land Beulah; for the Lord delights in you, and your land shall be married."

This teaching affirms that your season of desolation will be exchanged for joy, healing, and covenant fulfilment.

1. Hephzibah: You Are God's Delight – God delights in you, not based on what you've done, but who you are in Christ.
2. Beulah: Covenant Belongs to Your Land – Your land (spiritual, emotional, marital) is marked by promise and restoration.
3. Standing in Hope Is Not Passive – It's an act of faith that births restoration through surrender, intercession, and obedience.
4. Spiritual Barrenness Will Not Define You – God is turning the 'desolate' place into a fruitful covenant place.
5. You Are a Gatekeeper and Watchwoman – Your prayers are restoring broken walls (Isaiah 58:12).

Discussion:

What is your desolate place?
What promise are you reclaiming?'

Prophetic Activation:

"Lord, I receive my name as Hephzibah. I receive my land as Beulah. Let every desolate place be married to Your promise. I stand in covenant, and I will not be moved."

- What area of your life has felt forsaken or desolate?
- What promise are you standing on?
- What does covenant restoration mean to you?
- Which name or label has God removed from your identity?
- How do you feel like being called "His Delight" and "Bride of God"?
- Where have you seen God's faithfulness in your story?
- Write a declaration about your identity in Christ.

Please use your reflection journal to continue

Preparing a Ministry for Reconciliation

This session being the final session is to equip you as a disciple/leader with biblical understanding and practical tools for leading others in marriage and family reconciliation and women's emotional/spiritual healing.

Scripture Reference -
- **2 Corinthians 5:18–19**
- **Colossians 3:12–14**
- **Luke 15 (Prodigal Son)**
- **Romans 12:18**

The ministry of reconciliation is a divine assignment given by God to every believer to restore broken relationships between God and people and between people themselves. It's rooted in the heart of the Gospel: **healing, restoration and peace.**

What It Means Practically

- Restoring People to God - you become a bridge, pointing others to the love, mercy, and forgiveness of Jesus. (2 Corinthians 5:20)
- Healing Broken Relationships - this includes families, marriages, churches, and even cultures torn apart by offense, betrayal, or division. You carry God's heart to restore unity where the enemy has sown separation.
- Forgiving as Christ Forgave You - You model the mercy of Jesus, choosing grace over resentment, forgiveness over retaliation. (Ephesians 4:32)

Preparing for a Ministry of Reconciliation

Why It's Powerful
- It reflects the very mission of Jesus (Luke 4:18) to bind up the broken hearted
- It breaks generational cycles of pain and separation
- It brings the Kingdom of God into everyday life, homes, marriages, communities

For You Personally
As someone standing for marriage restoration, financial breakthrough and emotional healing, you are actively walking out this ministry. God is using
- Your intercession
- Your obedience
- Your willingness to forgive and wait in faith to restore not only your family, but to equip you to help restore others.

Preparing for a Ministry of Reconciliation

Restoration Pathway

- Repentance (return to God)
- Release (let go of bitterness & pain)
- Repair (embrace the process of healing)
- Rebuild (participate in restoration)
- Reconcile (walk in unity)

Healing Declaration

I am a vessel of restoration. I am not defined by the wounds I carry, but by the healing I release.
I declare that through Christ, I am whole, restored, and equipped to be a restorer of homes, hearts, and generations.

- Where do I need to experience reconciliation in my own life?
- Where has God healed me in ways I can now minister to others?
- Are there any wounds still influencing my relationships today?
- What is God asking you to restore?
- Who might need your forgiveness, encouragement or truth spoken in love?
- How can you model reconciliation in your own home or ministry?

Please use your reflection journal to continue

_____
_____
_____
_____
_____
_____
_____
_____
_____
_____
_____
_____
_____
_____
_____
_____
_____
_____
_____

Declarations

Redemption *for* My Marriage

"I put my hope in the Lord to redeem and restore my marriage. His mercy is abundant, and His redemption is assured."

Psalm 130:7-8

O Israel, hope in the Lord; for with the Lord there is mercy. and with Him is abundant redemption. And He will redeem Israel from all his sins.

Lord, I trust You to redeem all things concerning my marriage. Thank You for Your endless mercy which covers every sin and every season. My hope is in You alone to restore what has been broken. Let Your abundant redemption flow in my home. In Jesus' name, amen.

THE MINISTRY OF RECONCILIATION

All this is from God, who through Christ reconcilied us to himself and gave us the ministy of reconciliation; that is, in Christ God was reconciling the world to himself, not counting their trespasses against them, and entrusting to us the message of reconciliation. –2 Cor. 5:18–19 ESV

UNDERSTANDING RECONCILIATION

- Restoring people to a right relationship with God.
- Healing divisions and bringing peace to broken relationships.
- Forgiving others as God in Christ forgave us.
- Modeling unity and love through the gospel of Christ.

DECLARATIONS

- I am a minister of reconciliation.
- Through Christ, I bring restoration and forgiveness.
- I carry the message of unity and peace.

PRAYER

Father, thank You for reconciling me to Yourself through Jesus. Help me to be a messenger of Your love, healing, and forgiveness. Use me to bring reconciliation to others and to share the gospel of peace. Amen.

Facilitator's Notes

WOMEN ARE GOD'S DAUGHTERS AND HE LOVES THEM DEARLY.

THIS PROGRAMME AND WORKBOOK IS TO EMPOWER WOMEN TO UNDERSTAND THEIR TRUE IDENTITY IN CHRIST BECAUSE THAT IS THE ESSENCE OF THEIR FOUNDATION. THE FOUNDATION IN CHRIST PREPARES THEM FOR EVERY EVENTUALITY THEY FACE IN THEIR LIVES.
MY RELATIONSHIP WITH GOD IS THE BASIS BY HOW I LIVE, SO THAT IN ANY OF LIVES CHALLENGES, I AM ABLE TO DISCERN HOW HE HAS CALLED ME TO DEAL WITH THE SITUATION THAT BRINGS HIM GLORY. WOMEN, YOU ARE GOD'S GIFT TO THE WORLD

THIS PROGRAMME WILL OPEN YOUR EYES SPIRITUALLY TO YOUR RELATIONSHIP WITH GOD AND HOW TO ALIGN YOU WITH HIS PURPOSE FOR YOUR LIFE. AND FOR RESTORATION.

JACQUELINE ANI
PROGRAMME DIRECTOR &
FACILITATOR

THE STANDERS
DISCIPLESHIP &
MENTORSHIP
WORKBOOK

Client Testimonial

Thank you Jacqueline Ani ! This class has been life changing and transforming. The Holy Spirit touched me very early on but lack of knowledge and not really understanding what was happening, I wasn't always walking in obedience. This class, along with the Holy Spirit grounded me and grew me. Without it, I don't think I would have known how to move forward in many areas, not just marriage

Attending the Standers Discipleship Class has been a life-changing experience for me. Through this class, I've gained a deeper understanding of God's Word and discovered powerful truths about my identity in Christ. Scriptures that once seemed distant or hard to grasp have come alive, and I now walk with greater confidence in who I am as a daughter of the King. One of the most beautiful parts of this journey has been the fellowship with other women. What began as a class for standers in marriage has blossomed into genuine friendships and strengths to stand for God's word. Jacqueline, the class's founder, is such a blessing. She brings wisdom and patience to every session, but she also sets a high standard—and rightly so. Her heart is to see every woman equipped with the full armour of God, ready to stand firm in faith and walk boldly in their calling. She doesn't just teach; she leads by example, challenging us to go deeper, not settle for surface-level faith, and truly become disciples of Christ.
I've come away from this class not only knowing more about God, but also knowing more about myself—my purpose, my identity, and the power that comes from living in truth.

Motivational Gifts Test

Read each statement and rate it to the left of the number. When finished, transfer each question's rating onto the response sheet.

No Desire Toward it	Almost Never True	Sometimes True	Almost Always True
1	2	3	4

_____ 1. I am able to sense the direction God desires for His people to move and share it with others.

_____ 2. I enjoy pitching in on service projects in the church.

_____ 3. I am able to organize my thinking in such a way as to systematically present a Bible lesson to others.

_____ 4. People often come to me with their personal problems for counsel.

_____ 5. I enjoy giving to those in serious financial need.

_____ 6. People seem to respect me and follow my lead.

_____ 7. I have a tender heart toward the needy and will often do what I can to help those who are in distress.

_____ 8. I speak up for what is biblically right even when people think I am narrow-minded and oppose principles.

_____ 9. I usually volunteer to help with tasks that need to be done.

_____ 10. I enjoy diligent study so as to accurately teach the Word.

_____ 11. I enjoy encouraging those who are discouraged and down hearted.

_____ 12. I cheerfully give well above a tithe to the work of the Lord.

_____ 13. I am good at setting goals and seeing the direction a group of people should take.

_____ 14. I enjoy visiting the sick and shut-in.

_____ 15. I feel compelled to communicate God's message from the Word so people know what God expects of them.

_____ 16. I am willing to work at a task regardless of how simple or trivial it may seem.

_____ 17. Others comment on how much they have enjoyed, learned, or grown under my teaching.

_____ 18. I often challenge others to reach their potential in Christ.

_____ 19. I am known for my generosity and sometimes sacrificial giving.

_____ 20. I am able to guide and motivate people to join in the achievement of my goals.

_____ 21. I tend to look out for those who are neglected and alienated.

_____ 22. I am not afraid to announce God's judgment on sin.

_____ 23. I feel a sense of satisfaction in seeing a job through to completion.

_____ 24. I am able to thoroughly study Scripture and share my finding with others.

_____ 25. I make myself available total with others.

_____ 26. I often give anonymously to those in need.

_____ 27. If in a group where there is no leader, I will assume leadership.

_____ 28. I empathize with those who are embarrassed and humiliated and seek to comfort them.

_____ 29. I speak boldly and with conviction what I believe God wants people to know.

_____ 30. I am very dependable for getting things done.

_____ 31. I am able to make the Bible clear and relevant for others.

_____ 32. I encourage others to go on with the Lord.

_____ 33. I am willing to lower my standard of living in order to help out.

_____ 34. I am a goal setter.

_____ 35. I like to spend time with those who are lonely and hurting to cheer them.

Response Sheet for Seven Motivational Gifts Test

You must respond to each statement for the test to be valid. You must fill in your response of 1, 2, 3 or 4 for each question.

						Totals	
1.	8.	15.	22.	29.	=		A.
2.	9.	16.	23.	30.	=		B.
3.	10.	17.	24.	31.	=		C.
4.	11.	18.	25.	32.	=		D.
5.	12.	19.	26.	33.	=		E.
6.	13.	20.	27.	34.	=		F.
7.	14.	21.	28.	35.	=		G.

1. Put an asterisk or star next to the highest total. You may have more than one row totaling this same amount. Put an asterisk or star by each.
2. Match the letter next to the totals of those with an asterisk/star with the A-G code below.
3. Write the name of the gift(s) that match in the box at the bottom of this page. What is written may very well be the spiritual gift(s) of the person taking the test.

Note: if the highest total is under 10 for any gift, this test should probably be considered inconclusive. More ministry experience may be required in different areas of ministry. Very possibly the highest total may be the gift but totals of 10 or less should be seen as tentative.

4. If there are any totals with no more than a one-point gap from the highest total, yet still over ten, you may want to write that gift(s) down as a possible gift(s) as well. If however, you find that this yields more than three gifts, you probably should go with only the highesttotal as the more conclusive gift(s).

A= Prophecy	C = Teaching	E = Giving	G = Mercy
B= Service	D = Exhortation	F = Leadership	

173

Motivational Gifts Chart
Romans 12:3-8

The Gift	Description	Strengths	Pitfalls	Do it Right	Role Model
Prophecy	The eyes of the body; gifted with spiritual sight; say what they think; declare the truth; right or wrong, black or white; quality control; speak out about spiritual &/or social concerns in any setting.	See to the heart of the issue; motivated to reveal the truth; concerned with revealing a person's motives; has natural discernment.	Hard to keep silent when they feel truth is being twisted, hidden or offended; usually lack tact; doesn't always speak the truth in love; need to learn when to speak, who to speak to.	Approach life & others w/grace; learn that not everything needs to be said.	John the Baptist (Matt 3:1-12; 11:7-15)
Service/ Ministry	The hands of the body; meets physical needs; task oriented; have to do something to help.	Can see tasks that need to be done; always ready to serve; no task is too small.	Motives often misunderstood; can be easily offended if not appreciated; look down their noses at those who don't see other's needs; not able to say "no"; can isolate themselves behind the scenes; don't receive as well as give.	Remember who you are serving (God); recognize your specific area(s) of calling & be sure "good" things don't take away from it.	Martha (Luke 10 & John 12)
Teaching	The mind of the body; researches, instructs, communicates info for understanding & growth.	Motivated to validate truth; wants to know why, how, when, where; all about facts & details; asks questions.	Can be boring; have to tell you why they're qualified; over-value training & degrees; won't listen if you're not "qualified"; give too much info; can be easily offended & critical; can struggle to give practical application.	Be teachable.	Apollos (Acts 18:24-28) Aquila & Priscilla (Acts 18; Romans 16)
Exhortation/ Encouraging	The mouth of the body; cares for the spiritual needs of others; builds up; pep rally leader; encourages others; may or may not teach; meets specific need at specific time.	Not easily discouraged; on top of any situation.	Often won't let you grieve; can lack empathy; view things as "mind over matter"; can ignore the work of the Holy Spirit; talk a lot; pride in motivational skills; overload of people demands; offended if counsel not taken.	Remember that others are human just like you; remember that it is the kindness of Christ that draws people to Him.	Barnabas (Acts 4:36; 11:22-26)

The Gift	Description	Strengths	Pitfalls	Do it Right	Role Model
Giving	The arms of the body; gifted to produce & share resources (usually money); love to give, even if they don't have much; often frugal so they can give more; if they can't meet the need, they'll find another way to meet it.	Motivated to make money & give money; generous; caring; resourceful.	Can becomea stingy hoarder; can give away too much & neglect themselves; offended if you don't take their $ advice; debt/lack of $ plans offends them; equates love & value with gifts; critical of those who don't/can't give; use $ to control.	Remember that $is just a tool; if misused you ruin the tool & what you were using it on.	Dorcas (Acts 9)
Leading	The shoulders of the body; sees the big picture; gives direction; delegates; motivates others to get involved & meet goals; when there's no leader they'll step into the void; confident.	Instantly evaluates problem & assigns steps to solve it; delegates; adjusts as they go; vision; meets goals.	Can manipulate, control or dominate other's subconsciously; don't voice their appreciation; won't take your input; expects you to do your job; jump to conclusions; impatient; often change their minds; offended when not obeyed; can't stand turtles; upset if questioned.	Remember that a leader is the ultimate servant; lay down your life for your followers. You can't say "thank you" too much.	Nehemiah
Mercy	The heart of the body; sensitive; full of love, compassion, mercy; very forgiving; focused on emotional needs of others; shows caring with words and actions.	Compassionate; empathetic, loyal, forgiving, perceptive, consoling, non-judgmental.	Blind to other's faults; will take on the offenses of others; easily used; trouble seeing other's motives; trouble balancing mercy & justice.	Don't lose sight of the true needs of all: forgiveness & salvation. To lose sight of the goal is to lose sight completely. Exposure to those with the gift of exhortation can be helpful.	The Good Samaritan (Luke 10)

More information on spiritual gifts can be found at https://iblp.org/questions/what-are-seven-motivational-gifts.

Website for Manifestation Gift

Please visit the website below to take the test and view your results.

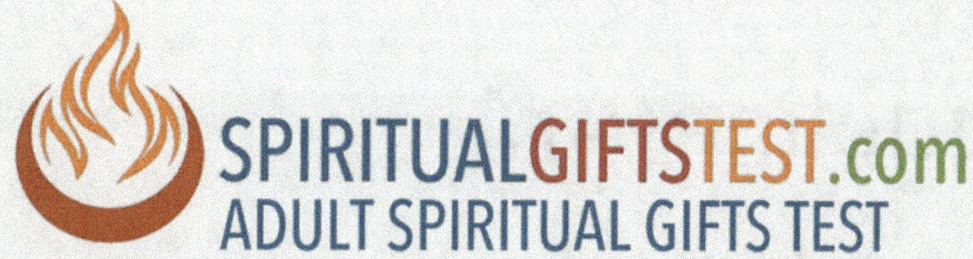

Thank-you!

Jacqueline Ani International

Contact:

jacquelineaniinternational.org
info@jacquelineaniinternational.org

www.ingramcontent.com/pod-product-compliance
Lightning Source LLC
Chambersburg PA
CBHW081421300426
44110CB00017BA/2339